The Relevance of Education

OTHER BOOKS BY JEROME S. BRUNER

Mandate from the People (1944)

Opinions and Personality (1956) with Smith and White

The Process of Education (1960)

A Study of Thinking (1962) with Goodnow and Austin

On Knowing: Essays for the Left Hand (1962)

Studies in Cognitive Growth (1966) with Olver and Greenfield

Toward a Theory of Instruction (1966)

Processes of Cognitive Growth: Infancy (1968)

Beyond the Information Given (1973) edited by Jeremy M. Anglin

The
Relevance
of Education

BY JEROME S. BRUNER
EDITED BY ANITA GIL

The Norton Library

W · W · NORTON & COMPANY · INC ·

NEW YORK

For Peter Dow

Copyright © 1973, 1971 by Jerome S. Bruner

First published in the Norton Library 1973

ALL RIGHTS RESERVED
Published simultaneously in Canada
by George J. McLeod Limited, Toronto

Books That Live
The Norton imprint on a book means that in the publisher's
estimation it is a book not for a single season but for the years.
W. W. Norton & Company, Inc.

Library of Congress Cataloging in Publication Data

Bruner, Jerome Seymour.
  The relevance of education.

  (The Norton library)
  Bibliography: p.
  1. Educational psychology. 2. Child study.
I. Title.
LB1051.B74   1973   370.15   73-941
ISBN 0-393-00690-5

Designed by Ruth Smerechniak

Printed in the United States of America

1 2 3 4 5 6 7 8 9 0

CONTENTS

Preface to the Norton Library edition

I would note three points in this Preface to the paperback edition of the *Relevance of Education*. The first is that many of the topics treated in this volume have been temporarily driven underground. I'm reminded of the title of a volume by Bertrand Russell: *Unpopular Essays*. Radical concern has for the moment moved far away from the explicit curriculum of education, concentrated instead on the implicit or "hidden" curriculum by the instrumentality of which bright students are often turned dull and, worse, poor students defeated. The utopian impulse has been toward the abolition of the ordinary school, the establishment of "free" schools or of "alternative" schools embodying the values of an "alternative" society.

I find myself rather in sympathy with this impulse to look again at the roots of our system of schooling. But I am somewhat constrained by the knowledge that however we transform the aims of education as a result of current reexamination, the mastery of skills will still be at the heart of the matter. It is their deployment that will be altered: their place in one's life, the ends to which they are put. But this does not reduce the importance of skill, its acquisition, the manner in which it is rendered flexible. My critics have accused me of being too intellectual in my approach to this issue. I confess my full guilt! It is, I think, like being too athletic about tennis or pole-vaulting: whatever role they may play in one's life or whatever the use to which one puts them, there remains the problem of how to get good enough to play at Wimbledon or to go over 17 feet. This is a very unpopular idea. I believe that striving for intellectual excellence and struggling for radical social change are not incompatible.

The second point has to do with a more general public fatigue with the issues of education. Schools and universities appear unruly, "youth culture" is feared by many and even despised by some. This has led to as extreme a stance toward education among spokesmen for the "Middle Americans" as the one taken by those disenchanted from the Left. One hears from some highly placed school officers, "Curriculum reform and new programs are anathema. Compensatory education is the only thing that is in." The mood is cautious, the tone rather anti-intellectual. Surely, "compensatory education" has been neglected with cruel effects on the victims who have failed the standard, middle-class oriented course. But for reasons that are endemic to the American educational scene, we tend to opt for one good at a time. Does an effort on behalf of those who have been wronged preclude continued attention to the cultivation of excellence among those who have *not* been victims?

Finally, some reviewers have read this volume not only as a change of heart since *The Process of Education*, but also as a change of theory. Change of heart, yes, in the sense that we can no longer take for granted the educational mission handed to the schools by the society. The task of giving heart to the discouraged, of rescuing those who have been excluded from the system—these are crucial. But with respect to mind and its cultivation, the process of empowering it with the instruments and structures of knowledge, of equipping it with powers and strategies for sifting and structuring information: these remain as crucial as ever they were.

JEROME S. BRUNER

Oxford, England
July 1972

PREFACE

This book is built around essays written between 1964 and 1970, years of deep and tumultuous change. They were disturbing years. They had an impact in their own right, amplified by my increasingly strong involvement during the period with very young human beings. These were my "subjects" in experiments and observations. The contrast between the exterior social turbulence and human helplessness I was studying kept imposing itself.

The period of these essays is the period of the elaboration of youth culture, with its concomitant revolt against "establishment schooling." It extends from Berkeley to Columbia, through the Harvard bust and the Sorbonne riots, to the Prague spring and summer and the beginnings of the long and cruel winter after. In our own universities, we have gone from the salad days of "new colleges" to the present "hard line" of so many faculties. The young began the period in political activism; then there was the sharp fire of a new extremism; now, in the early winter of 1971, it is a new disengagement.

Through the turmoil and idealism of these years has run

a theme of "naturalness," of "spontaneity," of the immediacy of learning through direct encounter. A distrust of traditional ways has brought into question whether schools as such might not be part of the problem—rather than a solution to the problem of education. American educational reform in the early '60s was concerned principally with the reconstruction of curriculum. The ideal was clarity and self-direction of intellect in the use of modern knowledge. There were brave efforts and successful ones in mathematics and physics, in chemistry and biology, and even in the behavioral sciences. The faltering of the humanists at that time was puzzling, though it later became clearer. A revision of the humanities involved too many explosive issues. In the second half of the decade, the period of these essays, deeper doubts began to develop. Did revision of curriculum suffice, or was a more fundamental restructuring of the entire educational system in order? Plainly, the origins of the doubt go deep and far back into the changing culture and technology of our times. But our ruinous and cruel war in Vietnam led many who would have remained complacent to question our practices and priorities. How could a society be so enormously wealthy, yet so enormously and callously destructive—while professing idealism? How wage a war in the name of a generous way of life while our own way of life included urban ghettos, a culture of poverty, racism, etc. We looked afresh at the appalling effects of poverty and racism on the lives of children and the extent to which schools had become instruments of the evil forces in our society. Eloquent books like Jonathan Kozol's *Death at an Early Age* began appearing.

It was the black community that first sought "free schools," freedom schools. They were to help black identity, to give a sense of control back to the community. Just as the civil rights movement provided models for social protest at large, so too the drive for free schools for the children of the black poor produced a counterpart response in the intellectual middle-class community. The revolt against the system very quickly came to include the educational Establishment. Generous-minded men like Ivan Illich and Paul Goodman, inveighing against the deadening bureaucratic hold of teachers and educational administrators, voiced a new romanticism: salvation by spontaneity, disestablish the established schools. It was a view that took immediate root in "In" youth culture.

But if romanticism was solace for some, despair was the order for others. By the spring of 1970, when Elizabeth Hall, one of the editors of *Psychology Today*, asked me what I thought about American education at the moment, all I could answer was that it had passed into a state of crisis. It had failed to respond to changing social needs—lagging behind rather than leading. My work on early education and social class, for example, had convinced me that the educational system was in effect our way of maintaining a class system —a group at the bottom. It crippled the capacity of children in the lowest socioeconomic quarter of the population to participate at full power in society, and did so early and effectively.

Harsh though these words were, I went on even further and expressed doubt about the further development of problem-solving curricula for the more intelligent kids. As she reported in *Psychology Today* (December, 1970), I went on: "At this point in history and perhaps at this time in my life I am looking for the social invention, however radical, that would make it possible for people to work together on our massive problems of poverty, urban life, learning to use the technology effectively."

It is not surprising, then, that this little volume, arranged roughly in chronological order, should begin with an essay that bears the title "The Perfectibility of Intellect" (vintage 1965) and end with one called "Poverty and Childhood" (a product of 1970).

But there is also a quieter and deeper conflict working itself out in the essays of these intense years. One limb of it is the conviction I hold about the structure and connectivity of knowledge. Our knowledge of the world is not merely a mirroring or reflection of order and structure "out there" but consists rather of a construct or model that can, so to speak, be spun a bit ahead of things to predict how the world *will* be or *might* be. A culture, moreover, equips its members with such structured models of the world so that they may predict, interpolate, and extrapolate. That much for knowledge. Without such models, man would not be the species he is. Nor would culture be so controlling.

But there is a second strain in these essays. It has to do with intention, with self-imposed direction. Its core is the idea of the selectivity imposed by action and purpose, the biasing effect these have on our knowing and on the uses of knowledge. As one moves through these essays, the emphasis on intention and selection becomes more insistent. It is an old story in my thinking. It was crucial to my earlier work on the role of selectivity in perception. It was a hallmark of the work on strategies for conceptualizing. And it emerges now in new form in the concept of intention discussed in the final essay of this volume. But interestingly enough, it is a concept that at most is implicit in the first three essays.

Perhaps the reason for this new "phasing in" is that my work during this period has gradually shifted away from concern with structured, conventional knowledge to a preoccupation with the opening two years of life. But it also is a reflection of my own doubts as to whether the conventional models, the forms of our knowledge are appropriate to our purposes in our times, that perhaps new requirements of action were proving the inadequacy of our models as they had emerged historically. So I have turned back to the role and structure of action and the origins of order in action and intention. The child first learns the rudiments of achieving his intentions and reaching his goals. En route he acquires and stores information relevant to his purposes. In time there is a puzzling process by which such purposefully organized knowledge is converted into a more generalized form so that it can be used for many ends. It then becomes "knowledge" in the most general sense—transcending functional fixedness and egocentric limitations.

The reader will find struggles and muddles throughout these essays, signs of the author's trying to deal with the structure of knowledge and the functions it serves or the purposes to which it is put. I plead the reader's patience.

I recall a delightful encounter with Niels Bohr during the war years that sustains me in my failure. It is quite cloak-and-dagger, if in a highbrow way. I used to go from Princeton to Washington in 1944 on Fridays to consult with a government agency. Indeed, I would go down by train on Thursday evenings, staying with Ruth and Richard Tolman overnight. So regular had the habit become that the Tolmans had provided me a key to their house. Richard Tolman was then Deputy Director of the National Defense Research Committee, which dealt, among other things, with the Manhattan Project and the making of the Bomb. One evening, I let myself in (noting only that two strange cars were parked outside, both occupied) and was greeted by a charming man who introduced himself as Mr. Baker, a fellow guest, and said he was expecting me, and that the Tolmans would be home shortly. I learned much later that he had within the preceding five days been smuggled out of Denmark and flown across the Atlantic.

We sat over drinks and talked. He said he was a physicist. I was intrigued by the line he followed. It was about complementarity in physics, how he had first thought of it in connection with having to punish his son for what was patently a misdeed. Could he, constrained both by his duty as father and by his fondness for his son, *know* his son *simultaneously* both in the light of love and in the light of justice? Were these not mutually non-convertible ways of knowing?

I confess I am puzzled in the same way now about the relationship between knowledge as detached (competence?) and knowledge as a guide to purposeful action (performance?). Much of the romance of modern radical criticism is that detached knowledge is meaningless, bourgeois, and establishmentarian. I doubt it. Yet those who study the *acquisition* of knowledge are surely aware to what extent its acquisition is governed by selective purpose and is thereby subject to bias. For all that, in any particular instance, knowledge transcends the uses to which it is put. What one *has* and how one *gets* it turn out to be quite different. And our educational philosophy had better consider both.

For an academic man essays usually represent responses

to invitations, and so too with the selections in this volume. Let me say a word about the invitations and their occasions.

"The Perfectibility of Intellect" was a lecture in 1965 on the occasion of the two hundredth anniversary of the birth of James Smithson, the donor of the Smithsonian Institution in Washington. The eleven essays on science, culture, and society that were delivered on that occasion are contained in the volume *Knowledge Among Men,* edited by Dillon Ripley, the Director of the Smithsonian Institution (New York: Simon and Schuster, 1966). Some essays come close to possessing their author in the writing and for several years after. This had that effect on me. Its elaboration would come close to a kind of intellectual autobiography.

"Culture and Cognitive Growth" was prepared in 1966 for publication in the volume *Handbook of Socialization Theory and Research,* edited by David Goslin (Chicago: Rand McNally, 1969) and was a collaborative effort with my longtime colleague Dr. Patricia Marks Greenfield. It was our effort to assess what the title expresses: how culture affects cognitive development. Some readers may find this chapter somewhat technical. It is necessarily so, for it is an assessment of a wide-ranging literature. The reader may wish to return to it after further reading in the book.

"The Growth of Mind" was delivered in its original version (*American Psychologist,* 1965, *20,* 1007–1017) as my Presidential Address to the American Psychological Association in 1965. In its present version it is quite drastically and properly reduced, to avoid overlap with many of the points made elsewhere in the volume. The Presidential Address was an effort to convince my fellow psychologists that education and pedagogy needed them. I hoped to persuade them that developmental psychology without a theory of pedagogy was as empty an enterprise as a theory of pedagogy that ignored the nature of growth.

"Some Elements of Discovery" was given at a conference organized in 1965 by the Committee on Education and Development of the Social Science Research Council, and later published in a volume edited by L. Shulman and E. Keislar entitled *Learning by Discovery* (Chicago: Rand McNally,

1966). The version that appears in this volume has been rather deeply edited. I was asked to participate, I assume, because I had, some years before, published a paper entitled "The Act of Discovery" (*Harvard Educational Review*, 1961), which had been interpreted as the basis for a "school of pedagogy" by a certain number of educators. As so frequently happens, the concept of discovery, originally formulated to highlight the importance of self-direction and intentionality, had become detached from its context and made into an end in itself. Discovery was being treated by some educators as if it were valuable in and of itself, no matter what it was a discovery of or in whose service. The essay attempts to remedy some of the misuse into which the concept had fallen.

"Toward a Disciplined Intuition" was a paper that I prepared jointly with Blythe Clinchy during the conference in 1965 sponsored by the U.S. Office of Education, under the general title *Learning About Learning* (J. S. Bruner, editor. U.S. Office of Education, Cooperative Research Monograph #15 [Washington: U.S. Government Printing Office, 1966]). The discussion of intuition contained in the present volume is an effort to follow up some of the thoughts contained in the chapter so entitled in my earlier *The Process of Education*.

"Culture, Politics, and Pedagogy" was prepared for presentation at a series of university-wide lectures at Harvard sponsored by the Graduate School of Education. It began as reflections on historically famous texts in educational theory that had been discussed in my seminar at Harvard in 1966–67. I think it reveals the extent to which the liberal intellectual in America was being got at by the changing atmosphere to which I alluded earlier. The original essay, again in a fuller form, appeared originally in the *Saturday Review* (May 18, 1968).

"The Psychobiology of Pedagogy" was given in a somewhat altered version as the Phi Beta Kappa lecture at Rockefeller University in 1969. It is a curious essay in which, plainly, the author is caught between trying to understand man biologically as a culture-using organism, and at the same time trying to understand him as a product of the very culture that he creates as external to himself. It has never been published before, and is published here with a certain reluctance.

"The Skill of Relevance or the Relevance of Skill" was prepared in late 1969 for presentation at a symposium in London, "Education in the '70s," sponsored by the *Encyclopaedia Britannica*. It is the essay in which the concept of skill re-emerges in my work after some years of absence, an emphasis as much on doing as on knowing. This essay also was published eventually in the *Saturday Review* (April 18, 1970).

"Poverty and Childhood" was prepared in 1970 while I was on sabbatical leave, presumably working on theories of motor development in early infancy. I did work on that topic, but I could not do so for long during that troubled year with much conviction. I wrote the essay in London and it was given as the Inglis Lecture at Harvard. Another version was presented on the occasion of receiving the Annual Award of the Merrill-Palmer Institute in Detroit.

I must say a word, finally, about the making of this volume. I worked closely with the editor, Mrs. Anita Gil. She is one of those perceptive editors who know with more perspective than the author how the pieces fit together. It has been a great and an enlightening pleasure working with her. One becomes much clearer about what one is trying to say. The author is grateful to Dr. Thomas Rowland for proposing that this volume be put together.

JEROME S. BRUNER

Cambridge, Massachusetts
January 1971

The Relevance of Education

1

The Perfectibility of Intellect

I shall concern myself in what follows with the vexed problem of the perfectibility of man's intellect. Let me consider the matter in the light of four constraints on the exercise of intellect. The first is the nature of knowing itself, as we observe it in intact human beings attempting to gain knowledge. The second derives from the evolution of intellect in primates, including man. The third constraint is imposed by the growth of intellect from childhood to such perfection as man may reach. The fourth has to do with the nature of knowledge as it becomes codified and organized in the society of learned men. It is too broad a task I have set for myself, but unavoidably so, for the question before us suffers distortion if its perspective is reduced. Better to risk the dangers of a rough sketch.

Let me confess that I, indeed any student of human intellect, can hardly pretend that what I say of the reach and range of human intellect is innocent of social, political, and moral consequences. For however one poses the problem, whatever one finds must inevitably affect or at least question our concept of what is humanly possible in the cultivation of mind. The issue of the perfectibility of intellect stirs passionate debate. Beware those who urge that the debate is without purpose, that the results of scientific inquiry carry self-evident implications with them. For it is a debate that requires continual renewal lest our educational enterprise fail to fulfill its function either as an agency for empowering human minds or as a reflector of the values of the culture. What the student of human intellect can do is to refresh the debate with estimates of what is possible and estimates of what is the cost of the possible.

THE NATURE OF KNOWING

Consider first the nature of human intellect as we understand it after a half century of investigation—investigation often more orderly than startling, yet of a nature that yields a steady knowledge. In most recent years, the quest has yielded more surprising turns as we have undertaken the job of forging compatible links between man's intellect and the computers that are its servants.

Perhaps the most pervasive feature of human intellect is its limited capacity at any moment for dealing with information. There is a rule that states that we have about seven slots, plus or minus two, through which the external world can find translation into experience. We easily become overwhelmed by complexity or clutter. Cognitive mastery in a world that generates stimuli far faster than we can sort them depends upon strategies for reducing the complexity and the clutter. But reduction must be selective, attuned to the things that "matter." Some of the modes of reduction require, seemingly, no learning —as with our adaptation mechanisms. What does not change ceases to register: steady states in their very nature cease to stimulate. Stabilize the image on the retina by getting rid of fine tremor, and the visual world fades away. There is another type of selectivity that reflects man's deepest intellectual trait and is heavily dependent on learning. Man constructs models of his world, not only templates that represent what he encounters and in what context, but also ones that permit him to go beyond them. He learns the world in a way that enables him to make predictions of what comes next by matching a few milliseconds of what is now experienced to a stored model and reading the rest from the model. We see a contour and a snatch of movement. "Ah yes, that's the night watchman checking the windows . . ." Or a patient sits before a physician complaining that vision in one eye is unaccountably dim. Both doctor and patient are involved in kindred activities. If the doctor diagnoses a scotoma, a deadened area on the retina, he does so by a process analogous to the process that leads the patient not to see a "hole" in his visual field, but a dimming, for the victim of a scotoma completes the hole by extrapolating what the rest of the eye is taking in. It is in the nature of the selectivity governed by these models that we come increasingly to register easily on those things in the world that we expect; indeed we assume that the expected is there on the basis of a minimum of information. There is compelling evidence that so long as the environment conforms to the expected patterns within reasonable limits, alerting mechanisms in the brain are quietened. But once expectancy is violated, once the world ceases strikingly to correspond to our models of it (and it must be rather striking, for we ride roughshod over minor deviations), then all the alarms go off and we are at full alertness, thanks to our neural reticular system. So man can not only deal with information before him, but go far beyond the information given— with all that this implies both for swiftness of intellect and for fallibility. Almost by definition, the exercise of intellect, involving as it must the use of short cuts and of leaps from partial evidence, always courts the possibility of error. It is the good fortune of our species that not only are we highly adept at correction (given sufficient freedom from time pressure), but also have learned to institutionalize ways of keeping error within tolerable limits.

The models or stored theories of the world that are so useful in inference are strikingly generic and reflect man's ubiquitous tendency to categorize. William James remarked that the life of mind begins when the child is first able to proclaim, "Aha, thingumbob again." We organize experience to represent not only the particulars that have been experienced, but the classes of events of which the particulars are exemplars. We go not only from part to whole, but irresistibly from the particular to the general. At least one distinguished linguist has argued in recent times that this generic tendency of human intellect must be innately human, for without it one could not master the complex web of categorial or substitution rules that constitutes the syntax of language—any language. Both in achieving the economy with which human thought represents the world and in effecting swift correction for error, the categorizing tendency of intelligence is central—for it yields a structure of thought that becomes hierarchically organized with growth, forming branching structures in which it is relatively easy to search for alternatives. The blunders occur, of course, where things that must be together for action or for understanding happen to be organized in different hierarchies. It is a form of error that is as familiar in science as in everyday life.

I do not mean to imply, of course, that man structures his knowledge of the world only by the categorial rules of inclusion, exclusion, and overlap, for clearly he traffics in far greater complexity, too. Witness the almost irresistible urge to see cause and effect. Rather, the categorial nature of thought underlines its rule-bound nature. The eighteenth-century assumption that knowledge grows by a gradual accretion of associations built up by contact with events that are contiguous in time, space, or quality does not fit the facts of mental life. There are spheres where such associative laws operate within limits, as, say, with material that is strange and meaningless (the psychologist's nonsense syllables, for example), but for the most part organization is a far more active process of imposing order—as by forming a hypothesis and then checking it to be sure.

In the main, we do the greater part of our work by manipulating our representations or models of reality rather than by acting directly on the world itself. Thought is then vicarious action, in which the high cost of error is strikingly reduced. It is characteristic of human beings and no other species that we can carry out this vicarious action with the aid of a large number of intellectual prosthetic devices that are, so to speak, tools provided by the culture. Natural language is the prime example, but there are pictorial and diagrammatic conventions as well, theories, myths, modes of reckoning and ordering. We are even able to employ devices to fulfill functions not given man through evolution, devices that bring phenomena into the human range of registering and computing: phenomena too slow to follow or too fast, too small or too large, too numerous or too few. Today, indeed, we develop devices to determine whether the events we watch conform to or deviate from expectancy in comprehensible ways. My colleague George Miller (1965) put it well, speaking about computers: "Mechanical intelligence will not ultimately replace human intelligence, but rather, by complementing our human intelligence, will supplement and amplify it. We will learn to supply by mechanical organs those functions that natural evolution has failed to provide."

The range of man's intellect, given its power to be increased from the outside in, can never be estimated without considering the means a culture provides for empowering mind. Man's intellect then is not simply his own, but is communal in the sense that its unlocking or empowering depends upon the success of the culture in developing means to that end. There is a sense in which, as Professor Lévi-Strauss has taught us, human intellect does not vary in power as a function of the means and technology available to it. For the use of amplifiers of mind requires, admittedly, a commonly shared human capacity, and each society fashions and perfects this capacity to its needs. But there is, I believe, a respect in which a lack of means for understanding one matter places out of reach other matters that are crucial to man's condition whatever his culture.

Let me add one final point. Human beings have three different systems, partially translatable one into the other, for representing reality. One is through action. We know some things by knowing how to do them: to ride bicycles, tie knots, swim, and so on. A second way of knowing is through imagery and those products of mind that, in effect, stop the action and summarize it in a representing ikon. While Napoleon could say that a general who thinks in images is not fit to command, it is still true that a thousand words scarcely exhaust the richness of a single image. Finally, there is representation by symbol, of which the typecase is language with its rules for forming sentences not only about what exists in experience but, by its powerful combinatorial techniques, for forming equally good ones about what might or might not exist. Each of these modes has its own skills, its own prosthetic aids, its own virtues and defects, and we shall encounter them again before we are done.

THE EVOLUTION OF PRIMATE INTELLIGENCE

The evolution of primate intelligence is only now beginning to be understood. The evidence today is that the full evolution of human intelligence required for its movement the presence of bipedalism and tool use in early hominids. It is subsequent to these developments that we find a sharp increase in man's cranial capacity and in the size of his cerebral cortex. But the logic of the situation and indirect evidence argues that the development of tool using itself required some prior capacity, however minimal. I have recently observed a film shot in a natural park in East Africa in which a chimpanzee is using a straw, properly wetted in spittle, to insert into a termite hill to extract these insects. A baboon is watching. When his turn comes he tears the termite hill apart. Tool using of the kind found in early hominids is quite plainly a program in which tools are substituted for manual operations in much the same way that the carpenter can substitute a chisel for his forgotten plane, or a knife or even a saw blade. The evidence indicates that the change in tools used in East Africa after the first stabilization of a chopping tool was not very rapid. What was probably more important was the range of programs or activities into which this tool was substituted.

But having said that much, it is well to note that it was not a large-brained hominid that developed the technical-social way of life of the human, but rather the tool-using, cooperative pattern that gradually changed man's morphology by favoring the tool user over the heavy-jawed, smaller brained creature who depended upon his morphology alone. I must comment in passing upon the emergence of tools made to pattern, in contrast to spontaneous tools. It is at this point in human evolution, place it at some multiple of 10^5 years ago, that man comes to depend upon a culture and its technical pool in order to be able to fill his ecological niche. The biologist Peter Medawar (1963) commented that it is at about this point that human evolution becomes sufficiently elaborated to merit being called Lamarckian and reversible, rather than Darwinian and irreversible. For what is now being transmitted, over and beyond the human gene pool, is a set of acquired characteristics passed on in the cultural pool of a people. The reversibility, of course, is attested to by many splendid ruins, ruins manned by descendants with genes indistinguishable from their ancestors.

It is folly to speculate about the birth date of language. It seems likely, however, that the capacity that made possible the development of human language, the abstractive, rule-producing gift, must also have had something to do with the programmatic nature of tool using with its rules of substitution. It is not plain how we shall ever be able to reconstruct the matter.

One further feature of the evolution of intelligence relates to impulse control. We have had, in the past decade, several impressive overviews of the evolution of mammalian sexuality, from the familiar laboratory rat, through the ubiquitous macaque monkey, through the great apes, to man. The picture that emerges in the transition from lower mammals through primates is one of decreasing control by the hormonal system and an increasing part played by early experience through intervention of the cerebral cortex. Even before the emergence of higher apes, hominids, and early man, there was a striking increase in control of sexual activity by the central nervous system. With man and his ability to symbolize, the role of the central nervous system is further increased. For what is most striking in the change in sexuality from higher primates to humans is the emergence of what anthropologists speak of as classificatory kinship. In place of the higher apes' sexual dominance and restricting tradition of remaining within a range, the human species seems early to have developed a pattern involving reciprocal exchange of women outward to neighboring groups, an exchange used in the formation of mutual alliances. The role of this more stable and reciprocal kinship pattern in the upbringing of young must now concern us.

Human beings have a more prolonged and dependent childhood than other primates. Present opinion concerning the origin of this condition is somewhat as follows. As hominids became increasingly bipedal, with the free hands necessary for tool using, there was not only an increase in the size of the brain, but also a requirement of a stronger pelvic girdle to withstand the impacting strain of upright walking. The increased strength of the pelvic girdle came through a gradual closing down of the birth canal, and an obstetrical paradox was produced: a larger brain, but a smaller birth canal for the neonate to pass through. The resolution seems to have been achieved through the cerebral immaturity of the human infant, not only permitting the newborn to pass through the reduced canal, but assuring a prolonged childhood during which the ways and skills of the culture could be transmitted. There are reasonable arguments to be advanced in favor of the view that the direction of evolution in the nervous system of primates from the lowly tree shrews through lemurs and tarsiers and monkeys on to the higher apes and man has been in the direction not only of more cerebral cortex and more tissue for the distance receptors, but also toward the evolutionary selection of immature forms. This tendency to neoteny, as it is called, is particularly notable in man, to the extent that the human brain more closely resembles the fetal brain of the gorilla in some respects than the adult brain of that great ape. And so, to take one index, the human brain is about a quarter of adult size at birth; in rhesus monkeys and gibbons, the job is about finished after six months. And so it is argued that human infancy with its more malleable dependency can be viewed as a prolongation of the fetal period of the earlier primates.

It is not simply the length and dependency of childhood

that increases in man, but also the mode of raising young to the requirements of communal life. Let me describe very briefly some salient differences in the free learning patterns of immature baboons and the children of a hunting-gathering group in a roughly comparable ecology—the !Kung Bushmen. Baboons have a highly developed social life in their troops, with well-organized and stable dominance patterns. They live within a range, protecting themselves from predators by joint action of the strongly built, adult males. It is striking that the behavior of baboon juveniles is shaped principally by play with their peer group, play that provides opportunity for the spontaneous expression and practice of the component acts that, in maturity, will be orchestrated into the behavior either of the dominant male or of the infant-protective female. All this seems to be accomplished with little participation by any mature animals in the play of the juveniles. We know from a variety of experiments how devastating a disruption in development can be produced in subhuman primates raised in a laboratory by interfering with their opportunity for peer-group play and social interaction.

Among hunting-gathering humans, on the other hand, there is *constant* interaction between adult and child, or adult and adolescent, or adolescent and child. !Kung adults and children play and dance together, sit together, participate in minor hunting together, join in song and story telling together. At very frequent intervals, moreover, children are party to rituals presided over by adults—minor, as in the first haircutting, or major, as when a boy kills his first kudu buck and goes through the proud but painful process of scarification. Children, besides, are constantly playing imitatively with the rituals, implements, tools, and weapons of the adult world. Young juvenile baboons, on the other hand, virtually never play with things or imitate directly large and significant sequences of adult behavior.

Note, however, that among the !Kung one virtually never sees an instance of "teaching" taking place outside the situation where the behavior to be learned is relevant. Nobody "teaches" in our prepared sense of the word. There is nothing like school, nothing like lessons. Indeed, among the !Kung there is very little "telling." Most of what we would call instruction is through showing. In the end, everybody in the culture knows nearly all there is to know about how to get on with life as a man or as a woman.

The change in the instruction of children in more complex societies is twofold. First of all, there is knowledge and skill in the culture far in excess of what any one individual knows. And so increasingly there develops an economical technique of instructing the young based heavily on *telling* out of context rather than *showing* in context. The result of "teaching the culture" can, at its worst, lead to the ritual, rote nonsense that has led generations of critics to despair. But school imposes indirect demands that may be one of the most important departures from indigenous practice. It takes learning, as we have noted, out of the context of immediate action just by dint of putting it into a school. This very extirpation makes learning become an act in itself, freed from the immediate ends of action, preparing the learner for that form of reckoning that is remote from payoff and conducive to reflectiveness. In school, moreover, one must "follow the lesson" which means one must learn to follow either the abstraction of written speech— abstract in the sense that it is divorced from the concrete situation to which the speech might originally have been related— or the abstraction of language delivered orally but out of the context of an on-going action. Both of these are highly abstract uses of language.

It is no wonder, then, that many recent studies report large differences between "primitive" children who are in schools and their brothers who are not: differences in perception, abstraction, time perspective, and so on.

THE GROWTH OF INTELLECT

Let me now describe very briefly some of the major aspects of intellectual growth as we observe it in the growing child. The first and most general thing that can be said is that it does not flow smoothly but rather in spurts of rapid growth followed by consolidation. The spurts in growth seem to be organized around the emergence of certain capacities, including intellectual capacities. These latter have about them the character of prerequisites: one thing must be mastered before the child can go on to the next. Many of them are directed to two ends: the maintenance of invariance and the transcending of momentariness in registration and response. Let me say a word about each.

By invariance, we mean the recognition of kinship and continuity in things that are transformed either in location or appearance or in the response they evoke. The child must first learn to distinguish that objects have a persistent identity beyond the identity endowed upon them by the action one takes toward them. He then learns that an object persists beyond one's visual or tactile contact with it so that out of sight is not out of mind and a new appearance is not a new thing. He must then travel the long road of decentration, as Piaget (who has taught us so much about mental development) calls it: being able to represent things not only from the egocentric axis, but from other vantage points, personally as well as geometrically. In time, the child moves (at least in our culture) from a representation of the world through action to a representation based very heavily upon the appearance of things. Water poured from a standard beaker into one that is longer and thinner is now said by the four-year-old to be more water because it is "taller than before." In time, the child recognizes that there is constancy across change in appearance. What he is doing in the process of mastering invariance is, of course, constructing increasingly stable models of the world, increasingly comprehensive ones capable of reducing the surface complexity of the world to the limits of his capacity for dealing with information. In good season, and always with help from the culture, the child develops models or modes of representation that are far more symbolic or linguistic in nature. The growth of invariance, then, takes place with development of the enactive, ikonic, and symbolic representations we examined earlier. Students of the developmental process agree in broad outline about this progress, though the details and the terminology differ as one travels west from Moscow to Geneva to Paris to Cambridge to Boulder to Berkeley.

With respect to transcending momentariness, let me illustrate by citing a child, age five, who said of the larger of two half-filled beakers that it was fuller than the other, a moment later that it was also emptier, and then a moment later in answer to a question that it could not be both fuller and emptier. He worked with a consistent logic and saw no contradiction. The logic was self-sufficient for each episode and the three in question were not put together to make possible the recognition of contradiction. The bigger glass was fuller because it appeared to have more water; the bigger was also emptier because it appeared to have more empty space; a vessel could not be both emptier and fuller because, to cite the product of the child's *Sprachgefühl*, "that's silly." Again, development provides models that permit the child to sense coherence over larger and larger segments of experience, time- and space-binding representations that permit wider ranges of connection.

Save in the artificial setting of the school, dominated as it is by telling and a lack of guiding feedback, there is an extraordinary property of self-reward about the act of learning during growth. The satisfaction of curiosity seems to be self-rewarding among all primates. So, too, the development of competence. More uniquely human, finally, is that mysterious process whereby human beings pattern themselves on another and gain satisfaction by maintaining the supposed standard of their model. The three self-rewarding processes provide a motor for growth that is stalled only by repeated failure or by an inability to determine how one is progressing at a task. This does not mean, of course, that what a child learns is what is most empowering of his capacities but, rather, what happens to be available. It is here that the innovation of school and teacher can be critically important.

THE NATURE OF CODIFIED KNOWLEDGE

Consider now the nature of codified knowledge as it might affect our views about the perfectibility of intellect. The past half century has surely been one of the richest as well as the most baffling in the history of our effort to understand the nature of knowledge. Advances in the foundation of mathematics and logic, in the philosophy of science, in the theory of information processing, in linguistics, and in psychology—all of these have led to new formulations and new conjectures.

Perhaps the greatest change, stemming principally from the revolutions in physics, is in our conception of what a theory is. For Newton, inquiry was a voyage on the sea of ignorance to find the islands of truth. We know now that theory is more than a general description of what happens or a statement of probabilities of what might or might not happen—even when it claims to be nothing more than that, as in some of the newer behavioral sciences. It entails, explicitly or implicitly, a model of what it is that one is theorizing about, a set of propositions that, taken in ensemble, yield occasional predictions about things. Armed with a theory, one is guided toward what one will treat as data, is predisposed to treat some data as more relevant than others. A theory is also a way of stating tersely what one already knows without the burden of detail. In this sense it is a canny and economical way of keeping in mind a vast amount while thinking about a very little.

Discussing the organization of thought, Whitehead remarks in *The Aims of Education,* "Mankind found itself in possession of certain concepts respecting nature—for example, the concept of fairly permanent material bodies—and proceeded to determine laws which related the corresponding percepts in nature. But the formulation of laws changed the concepts, sometimes gently by an added precision, sometimes violently. At first this process was not much noticed or at least was felt to be a process curbed within narrow bounds, not touching fundamental ideas. At the stage where we now are, the formulation of the concepts can be seen to be as important as the formulation of the empirical laws connecting the events in the universe as thus conceived by us." What is perhaps most important about this way of viewing theory is the attitude it creates toward the use of mind. We now see the construction of theory as a way of using the mind, the imagination, of standing off from the activities of observation and inference and creating a shape of nature.

It can also be said of knowledge that, though it is constrained by the very mode of its expression, it can be expressed in various modes. There is a continuity between knowing how to operate a seesaw, being able to describe a balance beam and cause it to balance with weights placed differentially on either side, knowing that three ounces at six inches from the center of the balance will be equal to six ounces at three inches or two ounces at nine inches or eighteen ounces at one inch, and finally, knowing Newton's conception of moments. This partial isomorphism between more and less abstract ways of knowing something, though it gives the appearance of great obviousness, has implications that are all too easily overlooked.

Let me comment on a point that preoccupied J. Robert Oppenheimer: the connexity of knowledge. There is an implosion of knowledge just as there is an explosion. As observations have become more numerous, the ways in which they may be integrated and connected by powerful theories have also increased. Where the danger lies, of course, is in the possibility that fewer men will come to know the larger and more comprehensive domains to which such theories can be related. But there is reason to question such an eventuality. For it may be that the technologies now being devised for storing, relating, and retrieving information may change the very texture of the intellectual community. Crude though its present conception may be, the idea of a society of scholars connected to a data base through computational devices and programs that can quickly retrieve related information, suggests that we may have automatic servants and assistants vital to the pursuit of connection. We can begin to envisage ways of making knowledge less inert and discrete than it is now, placed as it is on the shelves of libraries or within the pages of our journals. What is required is a means of constantly rearranging and reordering knowledge in a fashion to reflect the theoretical advances and hypotheses current in the intellectual community that uses the knowledge.

The disciplines of learning represent not only codified knowledge but ways of thought, habits of mind, implicit assumptions, short cuts, and styles of humor that never achieve explicit statement. Concentrations of these ways of thought probably account for the phenomenal productivity in ideas and men of, say, the Cavendish Laboratory under Rutherford or Copenhagen under Bohr. For these ways of thought keep knowledge lively, keep the knower sensitive to opportunity and anomaly. I draw attention to this matter, for studies in the history of knowledge suggest that deadening and banalization are also characteristics of knowledge once it becomes codified.

PERFECTING THE POWER OF THOUGHT

I have concentrated on right-handed knowledge and given short shrift to the left hand—to the disciplines of art, of poetry, of history, of drama, and of metaphysics. Several implications follow from the account that I have given that bear not only upon the perfectibility of man's intellect but also upon the process of its perfecting. Let me in conclusion, then, comment upon a few of these.

In speaking of the nature of intellectual functioning, its evolution, its growth, and its codified products, I have placed heavy emphasis upon the role of models or theories that human beings build to render the varieties of experience into some manageable and economical form. Man creates theories before he creates tools. His capacity and skill for catching the invariances of the world around him probably underlie not only his success as a tool user and tool maker but also his use of that powerful instrument for expression and thought: human language. His myths, his art, his ritual, his sciences are all expressions of this deep-lying tendency to explicate and condense, to seek steady meaning in capricious experience.

Many scholars in this country and abroad have been involved this past decade in what has come popularly to be called the "curriculum revolution," the effort to start children younger and more effectively on the way to grasping the more powerful ideas embodied in the learned disciplines. And indeed it is a revolution in at least one obvious respect: the union of men at the frontiers of knowledge with those charged with instructing the young, the two working jointly on the conver-
.sion of learning into a form comprehensible and nutritious to

the young. The effort is also recentering the work of psychologists and others concerned with the development of children, though we are only beginning to understand the means whereby intellectual development can be assisted. It is in this activity that I see á fresh approach to the perfectibility of intellect.

Once granted that a principal task of intellect is in the construction of explanatory models for the ordering of experience, the immediate problem then becomes one of converting the most powerful ways of knowing into a form that is within the grasp of a young learner. Let curriculum consist of a series of prerequisites in knowledge and in skill, to be mastered with a built-in reward in increased competence as the learner goes from one step to the next. Such a view assumes that for any knowledge or empowering skill that exists in the culture there is a corresponding form that is within the grasp of a young learner at the stage of development where one finds him— that any subject can be taught to anybody at any age in some form that is both interesting and honest. Once mastered in that appropriate form, the learner can go on to more powerful, more precise forms of knowing and of using knowledge. It is already reasonably clear that this can be done in mathematics and science—though we are very, very far from doing it well. But it is also the case that reading simpler poetry brings more complex poetry into reach, or that reading a poem once makes a second reading more rewarding.

The conception of a curriculum as an effort to go more deeply and more powerfully and more precisely into a body of knowledge before one risks traveling more widely carries with it a self-limiting but benign constraint. One must choose the subjects one teaches from domains of knowledge robust and deep enough to permit such revisits.

And invention is required if one is to proceed in this way. How convert knowledge into the form that is within the grasp of a learner, so that he may be tempted on? Recall the three modes of knowing, characteristic of human cognitive operations —by action, by image, and by symbol. One approach to the task that has proved moderately successful is to begin a sequence of learning with an enactive representation—learning inertial physics by operating levers, learning music by composing and playing in a highly simplified musical notation, and so on. One goes beyond that to intuitive, image-laden forms, as with intuitive geometry or the kind of visual aids by which formal logic can be rendered in Venn diagrams, and finally to the increasingly abstract symbolic modes of a field of learning.

A more difficult task is to instill early in the learner what in effect is a balance between impatience with the trivial as proof against clutter and an open spirit toward what might be but is not obviously relevant. Here again, the experience of those who have worked on constructing curriculum suggests that one plunge right in. Short of that, it is difficult to accomplish anything. One starts concretely trying to give some feeling for the way of thought that is a discipline and one often succeeds. Again, it is as with musical instruction where one gives the learner the simplest possible Mozart rather than a scale so that as early as possible he may sense what music is.

Above all, what emerges from the past decade of experimenting with instruction is the importance of increasing the child's power of thought by inventing for him modes of access to the empowering techniques of the culture. The nature of a school as an instrument for doing this is very unclear. The perfecting of intellect begins earlier than we thought and goes communally from the outside in as well as growing from within. Perhaps the task of converting knowledge into a form fit for this function is, after all, the final step in our codification of knowledge. Perhaps the task is to go beyond the learned scholarship, scientific research, and the exercise of disciplined sensibility in the arts to the transmission of what we have discovered. Surely no culture will reach its full potential unless it invents ever better means for doing so.

2

Culture and Cognitive Growth

What does it mean, intellectually, to grow up in one cultural milieu and not another? It is, of course, a form of the old question of how heredity and environment relate: How, in this case, does intellectual development depend upon external influences; in what respects is it a series of unfolding maturational states? But the question is now in qualitative terms. The older debate on heredity versus environment was without a possible solution. For there is no psychological phenomenon without a biologically given organism nor one that takes place outside an environment. But we can, nevertheless, study the intersect in growth of biological background and cultural milieu with the more modest aim of learning what kinds of cultural difference make an intellectual difference at what points in development and how it comes about in some particular way.

It is not a new idea that cultural variation yields variation in modes of thought. It is a persistent theme in anthropology (for example, Boas, 1938; Mead, 1946; Whorf, 1956). Psychologists have also interested themselves in cultural influences on cognitive development. However, the methods used have rarely been equal to the task at hand. Anthropology's most recent and most promising approach, ethnoscience, explores qualitative cognitive variation by exploring the native terminology used for a particular objectively definable domain such as plants or disease or kinship (Sturtevant, 1964). Ethnoscience is limited as a method for investigating cognitive processes precisely because it does not deal with *processes* at all but with intellectual *products* as embodied in language. Like the older anthropological strategy of inferring living cognitive processes from static cultural products such as myth, ritual, and social life (for example, Durkheim and Mauss, 1963; Lévi-Strauss, 1962), ethnoscience infers the mind of the language user from the lexicon he uses. When we know the culturally standard system for kinship or disease classification we still do not know how the system developed or how it is used in novel situations. It is a bit like studying the growth of logic and thought in children of our own society through an analysis of grammar or logic in the books found in the library. It may help to define the idealized version of logical thought in the culture to do this. But it can tell little about the processes involved. In this respect, it is somewhat like some contemporary efforts to found psycholinguistics on the assumption that the rules underlying grammatical competence are the same as the laws that govern the production of grammatical sentences by native speakers. The laws governing the production of sentences may or may not be the same as the rules of grammar that are used to describe the correct combinations in the language.

In the 1930s and 40s psychologists carried IQ tests around the world. They had learned little more than that "natives" fared worse than standardization groups at home when projective tests came into vogue in the 50s (Lindzey, 1961) and cross-cultural attention shifted from intellect to affect. Again, the intrinsic value of intelligence tests was limited, abroad as at home, by the fact that the IQ is not a *process* but the product of many complex cognitive processes that other methods would have to unravel—and a product closely geared to school achievement in Western European culture at that. An ideological factor further complicated this work. As Strodtbeck (1964) points out, you can "prove" the power of heredity if you assume your test is "culture-free" (for example, Porteus' maze), whereas differences are due to environmental factors on the assumption of a "culturally relative" test. The assumption in a particular study probably reflected personal bias more than any other factor. Later, the absurdity of this distinction, parallel to that of choosing between heredity and environment, became evident.

The point of view animating the present discussion is that intelligence is to a great extent the internalization of "tools" provided by a given culture. Thus, "culture-free" means 'intelligence-free." Such a view of cognitive development has been put forth elsewhere (Bruner, 1964). Here we shall examine it by comparing intellectual development in cultures with radically different technologies.

One of the most interesting and oldest lines of cross-cultural work in cognition is through the study of sensation and perception. More than one intelligence tester noted that performance tests often seemed to put foreigners at as much of a disadvantage as verbal tests, and was forced to conclude that perceptual as well as verbal habits could vary radically from culture to culture (Cryns, 1964; Jahoda, 1956; Wintringer, 1955). If this were so then the study of perception could be fundamental in understanding any psychological process involving a response to the outside world.

The classical work on perception was done by the Cambridge Anthropological Expedition to the Torres Straits in 1901–1905. A famous and intriguing finding was that of Rivers (1905) concerning the lesser susceptibility of the Murray Islanders to the Müller-Lyer illusion.

The Todas of India yield a similar finding. This result has been interpreted to mean that the Todas, unaccustomed to in-

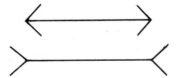

ferring three dimensions from two-dimensional displays, were less subject to the illusion; for as soon as three-dimensional stimulus materials were used, cultural differences disappeared (Bonte, 1962).

This work—suggesting the effect of *particular* cultural conditions such as the absence of pictures—has been followed up with studies of illusions in new places (for example, Allport and Pettigrew in South Africa, 1957) and by carefully controlled experimentation with line drawings. The latter studies have shown the interpretation of Rivers' work to be a correct one (Hudson, 1960). The effects obtained appear to depend upon perceptual *inference;* members of different cultures differ in the inferences they draw from perceptual cues, not in the cues they are *able* to distinguish. Such an interpretation suggests the value of studying more directly the way in which the cues are assimilated to different schemata in different cultures with the effect of producing large cultural differences. It is conceivable that one can also find differences in the cues most likely to be used in organizing percepts, given sufficiently complex stimulus fields. This is to say that, given complex input, the principles of selectivity will vary from culture to culture. This was certainly the point of the Cambridge studies under Rivers and of the careful observations of Bogoras in his work among the Chukchee (1904).

Our own cross-cultural work has followed other lines, lines of more recent historical development. We have asked first the naive question: Where in a culture should one find differences in the processes of thought? The anthropological linguists (for example, Whorf, 1956) suggested a concrete answer; where there are language differences there may (or should?) be cognitive differences. Our results have led us away from the parallelism of Whorf toward the instrumentalism that is more typical of Vygotsky (1961) and Luria (1961). Language as a tool and a constraint on cognitive development will be discussed below in more detail.

Most psychologists who work on development are strongly influenced by Piaget. But although Piaget has given us our richest picture of cognitive development, it is one that is based almost entirely on experiments in which age alone is varied. While he admits that environmental influences play a role, the admission is *pro forma,* and inventive experiments remain confined to Western European children, usually middle-class children at that. Where Piaget's work has been extended to non-Western societies, the emphasis has been almost entirely quantitative. Such work has been confined largely to timetable studies, to the time "lag" in the development of "foreign" children in contrast to children in Geneva or Pittsburgh or London (Flavell, 1963). A series of experiments carried out by the Harvard Center for Cognitive Studies has explored the role of culturally transmitted technologies in intellectual growth by the use of instructional techniques and cross-cultural studies (Bruner, Olver, Greenfield, et al., 1966). By comparing children of different ages in extremely different cultures we can ask the developmental question in its most radical form.

The focus, in what follows, is on two kinds of cultural constraints operating in development: value orientation and language. They seem fruitful for organizing the findings and illustrating the problems involved.

VALUE COMPLEXES AND COGNITIVE GROWTH

Let us, in the interest of specificity, limit the discussion of value orientations to the cognitive implications of one particular value contrast: collective *versus* individualistic orientation. Kluckhohn (Kluckhohn and Strodtbeck, 1961), in her studies of basic value orientations, attests to the fundamental nature of such a "decision" about orientation, commenting upon its importance for individual coping as well as for social solidarity. This value contrast represents more than alternate ways of seeing how things ought to be. Rather it reflects a contrast in how things *are*—a matter of world view about origins and existence and not merely a normative matter.

We begin with a series of studies carried out by Greenfield (Bruner, et al., 1966) in Senegal, the westernmost tip of former French West Africa in 1963–1964. These studies explored two main areas of cognitive development: concept formation and conservation in the classic Piagetian sense. The two areas complement each other nicely, for much of intellectual growth can be summarized as the development of equivalence or conservation, the equivalence rule of concepts being more "internal" and that of conservation more "external" in orientation. The subjects in both sets of experiments were all Wolof, members of the country's dominant ethnic group. The children were constituted into nine groups, better to discern the effect of cultural differences—three degrees of urbanization and education were represented, with three age levels within each.

The cultural milieu of our first group, rural unschooled children and adults, had neither schools nor urban influence. Although their traditional Wolof village had an elementary school, they had never attended it. The three age groups were: six- and seven-year-olds, eight- and nine-year-olds, and eleven- to thirteen-year-olds. There was also a group of adults.

The second major group—the bush school children—attended school in the same village or in a nearby village. This group was partitioned among first graders, third graders, and sixth graders, corresponding as closely as possible to the three age levels of the unschooled groups.

The third major group comprised city school children. These children lived in Dakar, Senegal's cosmopolitan capital and, like the second group, included first, third, and sixth graders. All the children were interrogated in Wolof, although French was the official language of instruction.

Returning now to the question of collective and individualistic orientations, we find that they have cognitive manifestations so basic as to render certain experimental procedures possible or impossible. In both the conservation and the concept experiments, the children were asked to give reasons for their answers. With both American and European children this type of question is usually put something like this: "Why do you say (or think) that thus and such is true?" Specifically, in a conservation problem, a child might be asked: "Why do you say that this glass has more water than this one?" But this type of question would meet with uncomprehending silence when addressed to the unschooled children. If, however, the same question were changed in form to "Why *is* thus and such true?" it could often be answered quite easily. It would seem that the unschooled Wolof children lack Western self-consciousness: they do not distinguish between their own thought or statement about something and the thing itself. Thought and the object of thought seem to be one. Consequently, the idea of explaining a *statement* is meaningless; it is the external event that is to be explained. We might expect from all this that the relativistic notion that events can vary according to point of view may be absent to a greater degree than in Western culture. This expectation is confirmed in Greenfield's concept formation studies, where the unschooled children can group a given set of objects or pictures according to only one attribute although there are several other possible bases of classification. Let it be noted that the Wolof *schoolchildren* do not differ essentially from Western children in this respect. It appears that school tends to give them something akin to Western self-consciousness, for they can answer questions implying a distinction between their own psychological reactions and external events; and, as they advance in school, they become increasingly capable of categorizing the same stimuli according to several different criteria or "points of view."

Piaget (1930) has proposed that intellectual growth begins with an egocentric stage, based on the inability to make a distinction between internal and external. This stage is then followed by a more developed egocentrism in which inner and outer are distinguished but confused. When inner psychological phenomena are attributed to inanimate features of the external environment, we have "animism"; when psychological processes are given characteristics of the inanimate, external world, we speak of "realism." These two tendencies are supposed to be complementary and universal forms of childish thought. Their mutual presence indicates a preliminary distinction between inner and outer.

In contrast to this formulation, one may propose that in traditional, collectively-oriented societies this distinction *never* gets made, that the world stays on one level of reality, and that this level is *realistic* rather than *animistic*. Animism has often been considered the characteristic of "primitive" thought par excellence. Quite possibly it is only the "powerful," well-cared for, competent child who sees the world in the pattern of his own feelings, and not the malnourished child of many traditional subsistence cultures like the Wolof. Kardiner (1965), too, has made this point with respect to the psychoanalytic conception of the "omnipotence of thought," noting that it is only where the child's every whim is satisfied that he is led to believe his thought omnipotent. The claim here is more severe. It is that animism does not develop where there is no support given for individualistic orientation. The argument would be that the child is not cognizant of his own psychological properties, does not differentiate these from properties of the physical world, and is therefore not cognizant of any psychological properties—far be it from him to attribute such properties to *inanimate* objects. In place of the cultivation of individual subjectivity, there is instead a reinforcing of the idea of "reality," "people-in-a-world-as-a-unity."

Consider the following evidence in support of this point. In an equivalence experiment done in the United States by Olver and Hornsby (Bruner, et al., 1966), children were shown an assortment of pictures and asked to put the similar ones together. They were then asked the reasons for their groupings. Children as they grow older form groups increasingly by the rule of superordinate grouping (those things go together that share a common attribute). The earlier pattern is more complexive in the sense that things go together because they fit into a story together, or whatnot. The transition from the earlier to the later mode of grouping is handled by "egocentrism." Things are alike by virtue of the relationship that "I" or "you" have to them, or the action taken toward them by "I" or "you." This is the picture in the United States. But Reich (Bruner, et al., 1966), using parallel techniques with Eskimo children in Anchorage, Alaska, finds that they do not express the function of things in terms of personal interaction with them nearly so often as do the American children of European descent. The Eskimo value system stresses self-reliance, but strongly suppresses any expression of individualism as an attitude toward life. The Eskimos are a subsistence culture that requires group action in its major forms of activity—sealing, caribou hunting, stone weir fishing. Eskimo children develop their superordinate structures without the intervention of the kind of egocentrism we observed in European children. Thus, such egocentrism cannot be a universal stage, not even in the development of superordination. Instead, it appears clearly relative to cultural conditions and values.

It should be clear by now that the kind of implicit egocentrism where one cannot distinguish different personal viewpoints, the kind that we have been calling *realism*, is strikingly different from the type that explicitly relates everything to oneself. Indeed, an explicit concept of self implies some sort of idea of not-self, for every concept must be defined as much by what it excludes as by what it includes. Or, to use Piaget's terminology, one could say equally well that an undifferentiated egocentrism that ends in realism is diametrically opposed to the kind that ends in "artificialism," the tendency to see all physical phenomena as made by and for men. This tendency is closely related to animism. It is the artificialistic type of egocentrism that appears in Olver and Hornsby's experiments and is probably typical of individualistically oriented industrial societies.

Unselfconscious realism was clear at yet another point in the Senegalese experiments. Here, too, one sensed its origin in the absence of control over the inanimate world characteristic of indigenous societies. In the classic experiment on the conservation of a continuous quantity (Piaget, 1952), one of two identical beakers was filled with water to a certain level. The Wolof child poured an equal amount in the second beaker. Then the experimenter poured the water from one beaker into a longer, thinner beaker, causing the water level to rise. The child was then asked if the two beakers contained the same amount of water or if one had more than the other and why. He was then asked for a reason. A type of reason in support of non-conservation judgments appeared that we had not seen before among American children (Bruner, et al., 1966), although Piaget (1952) reports one example in a Swiss four-year-old. This was the "magical" action reason: the child would say, "It's not the same" because "you poured it." The shift from equality to "inequality" was being resolved and justified by recourse to the experimenter's action. A natural phenomena was being explained by attributing special "magical" powers to intervening human agents. More likely, as Köhler (1937) points out, this as well as other cases of magical causation are made possible by realism in which animate and inanimate phenomena occupy a single plane of reality. That is, the child in the conservation experiment is faced with the following sequence of events: (1) water a certain way, (2) experimenter's action, (3) water changed. When the child says the amount is not the same because the experimenter poured it, he is basing his causal inference on contiguity—the usual procedure even in our society. But under ordinary circumstances, we would accept an explanation in terms of contiguous physical events *or* contiguous social events, but not a causal chain that included *both* kinds of event. Thus, "magic" only exists from the perspective of a dualistic ontology.

Note well that school suppresses this mode of thinking with astonishing absoluteness. There is not one instance of such reasoning among either bush or city Senegalese children who have been in school seven months or longer. Once again school seems to promote the self-consciousness born of a distinction between human processes and physical phenomena.

One can argue that just as soon as the child is endowed with control in the situation, his realism and magical reasoning will disappear. And so it turned out to be. The experiment was done again; everything remained basically the same with one exception: this time the child did *all* the pouring himself. Would he find yet another "magical" explanation for the seeming inequality of the water? Or, indeed, would he be as likely to believe that the water in the two beakers was uneven? Probably not. For while the child would be perfectly willing to attribute "realistic" powers to an authority figure like the experimenter, the child would not attribute any special powers to himself for his experience had taught him that he had none.

This suspicion was well confirmed by the results. Among the younger children, two-thirds of the group who transferred the water themselves achieved conservation, in contrast to only one-quarter of the children who had only watched the experimenter pour. Among the older children, the contrast was equally dramatic: eight in ten of those who did the pouring themselves, as compared with slightly less than half of the others, achieved conservation. When the child poured himself, his reasons were dramatically different from those given when an adult was pouring. Magical-action virtually disappears when the unschooled children themselves pour. What emerges instead are identity reasons—reference to the initial state of the system. The child who pours on his own now uses his initial equalizing operation as the basis for his justification of conservation: "They were equal at the beginning."

Price-Williams' (1961) study of conservation among Tiv children in Nigeria lends further weight to the point. He found that all of the Tiv children had achieved conservation of both continuous and discrete quantity by age eight, in sharp contrast to our upper limit of 50 per cent with much older Senegalese children. The description given by Price-Williams of the children's behavior during the experiments indicates that Tiv culture is quite different from Wolof in promoting an active manipulative approach to the physical world. He describes the children's behavior like this: "These children would spontaneously actually perform the operation themselves. . . . Furthermore, they would reverse the sequence of operations by, for example, pouring back the earth from the second container to the first." Such self-initiated action was *never* observed among unschooled Wolof children and may well be the key to the great disparity between the two cultures in spontaneous conservation results.

It may be that a collective, rather than individual, value orientation develops where the individual lacks power over the physical world. Lacking personal power, he has no notion of personal importance. In terms of his cognitive categories, now, he will be less likely to set himself apart from others and the physical world, he will be less self-conscious at the same time that he places less value on himself. Thus, mastery over the physical world and individualistic self-consciousness will appear together in a culture, in contrast to a collective orientation and a realistic world view in which people's attitudes and actions are not placed in separate conceptual pigeonholes from physical events.

This formulation is commonsensical; absence of personal mastery over the world is consonant with a collective orientation. And, indeed, we have observed empirically that the very same Wolof children who lack self-consciousness when questioned about their "thoughts" also seem to be hindered by a lack of experience in manipulating the physical world when they approach a problem relating to the conservation of quantity across transformations in its appearance.

Is there, however, developmental reason for this dichotomy between individual mastery and a collective or social value orientation? How does each come about? Is there a point in child-rearing at which a choice is made? Rabain-Zempléni (1965) has studied the fundamental ways in which the Wolof child, in his traditional bush setting, relates to the world of animate and inanimate things around him from the time of his weaning (age two) to his integration into a peer group (age four). Her findings confirm the preceding interpretation of later intellectual development among Wolof children and elucidate in a most dramatic fashion the antecedents of these developments in terms of child training practice and infant experience. Her work suggests that there is a developmental reason for the dichotomy between physical mastery and a collective orientation and that it appears at the very beginning of life. We learn that, "In a general way, motor manifestations of the child are, from the first year of life, not treated as productions existing for themselves in their capacity of exercising nascent functions, but already are interpreted as signifying a desire on the part of the child oriented in relation to some person."

So it seems as if adult members of a family evaluate and interpret the child's emergent motor activity either in terms of the relation of this activity to the people around him or in terms of motor competence per se, depending on the culture to which they belong. The child's attention must therefore be turned toward one or the other of these facets of physical activity. If, as in the Wolof case, the child's activity is not evaluated per se but in terms of its relation to group members, then one would expect both less mastery of physical acts and less differentiation of the physical from the social, that is, a "realistic" world view. Thus, adult interpretation of the child's first actions would seem to be paradigmatic for the choice between an individualistic and a collective orientation; for a social interpretation of an act not only relates the actor to the group but also relates the group, including actor, to physical events. When, on the other hand, acts are given an interpretation in terms of motoric competence, other people are irrelevant, and the act is separated, moreover, from the motivations, intentions, and desires of the actor himself.

Now back to the Wolof to trace a more complete developmental sequence in a collectively oriented culture. Rabain-Zempléni's naturalistic observations confirm the hypothesis, derived from the conservation behavior of the unschooled children, that Wolof children lack manipulatory experience, for she notes that manipulation of objects is an occasional and secondary activity for the child from two to four and that, furthermore, the Wolof child's "self image does not have to rest in the same way as in Europe on the power which he has over objects, but rather on that which he has over other bodies." She also notes that verbal interchanges between children and adults often concern the relations which are supposed to exist between people but rarely concern explanations of natural phenomena.

At the same time as the Wolof child's manipulation of the physical, inanimate world fails to be encouraged in isolation from social relations, the personal desires and intentions which would isolate him from the group are also discouraged. Thus, a collective orientation does not arise simply as a by-product of individual powerlessness vis-a-vis the inanimate world but is systematically encouraged as socialization progresses. Western society recognizes individual intention and desire as a positive function of age. According to Rabain-Zempléni, Wolof society does the reverse: the newborn child is treated as a person full of personal desire and intention; after he reaches the age of two, the adults in his milieu increasingly subordinate his desires to the ends of the group; he becomes less and less an individual, more and more a member of a collectivity.

When the social and physical constitute but a single level of reality, neither type of explanation should take precedence. To those who give precedence to physicalistic explanations, however, it may often appear that traditional peoples emphasize the social. This impression may be exaggerated by the fact that they often have greater knowledge about the social than the physical realm. Since a social explanation is considered perfectly adequate, we would not expect such people to press on for a physical account.

Gay and Cole's (1967; Gay, 1965) research among the Kpelle of Liberia furnish many other indications of the way in which people-as-causative-agents can play an extraordinary role in the traditional structure of knowledge. In school, facts are true because the teacher says them, and so there is often no attempt at understanding other reasons why or proving the fact for oneself. This same observation has been noted many places in Africa, for example, by D. Lapp (personal communication, 1965) in Cameroun. His experience was similar in this respect, for he found that the way to combat this tendency in teaching natural sciences was to have the students rather than the teacher do the demonstrations.

One other example from Cole and Gay. Among the Kpelle, arguments are won when they are unanswerable. Again, the ultimate criterion is social—does the other person have a comeback?—rather than "objective" or external. What is being argued about takes a back seat to the arguers.

Most intriguing is Rabain-Zempléni's observation that in the natural situation of sharing a quantity among several persons, a situation not too different from the second half of the conservation experiment where a quantity is divided among six beakers, more attention is paid to which person receives the substance at what point in the distribution than to the amount received. It is like their conservation explanations: more attention is focused on the person pouring—the social aspect of the situation—than on the purely physical aspect, the amount of water.

What is most interesting is the fact that, on a broader cultural level, this very same quality has been recognized by the poets of *négritude* or the African Personality as setting off black

from white. Lilyan Kesteloof (1962) in her book on Aimé
Césaire, the originator of the concept *négritude*, contrasts its
elements with the "valeurs-clef" of Western civilization. In opposition to "l'Individualisme (pour la vie sociale)" of European
cultures she places, "solidarité, née de la cohésion du clan
primitif." Leopold Sédar Senghor, poet and President of
Senegal, defines *négritude* in more psychological terms as "participation du sujet à l'objet, participation de l'homme aux forces
cosmiques, communion de l'homme avec tous les autres
hommes."

This complex, moreover, is held to be found in all African
societies and to stem from common cultural features. The
strong element of collective or social values is particularly clear
in the modern concept of African socialism which, unlike Western socialism, is supposed to be a mere modernization of existing ideals and social conditions rather than a radical revolution.

We have come far afield from intellectual development, but
what is so intriguing about these world views and ideologies
is that they should be so strongly reflected in the details of
cognitive growth. Bear in mind, however, that the distinctions
proposed here are not all-or-none, although they have been so
presented for the sake of clarity. The evidence, furthermore, is
thus far all from Africa. It is interesting that many different
ethnic groups should seem to have so much in common, but on
the other hand, we do not know to what extent this social or
collective orientation may be typical of all nonindustrial, traditional, or, perhaps, oral cultures. It is not certain that it is even
a valid description for every African society. Finally, although
we started out talking about the ramifications of a social or
collective orientation, we do not really know what causes what
in the whole complex of features that we have ended up discussing.

LANGUAGE AND COGNITIVE GROWTH

Our second cultural constraint is language. What does it
mean intellectually to speak one language rather than another?
What does it mean to write a language as well as to speak it?

Language at the highest level of generality can be divided into two components, a semantic and a syntactic. Most experiments attempting to relate language to thought have emphasized the semantic side in the style of Benjamin Lee Whorf (1956). Here the linguistic variable is the *richness* of the lexicon that a language has available to represent a given domain. Implicitly, but not explicitly, these experiments deal with the vocabulary of any one language *at a single level of generality* —its words rather than any structural relation among them.

A second kind of semantic linguistic variable is more structural. It deals with the *number of levels of generality* that can be encoded by the lexicon of a given language for a particular domain. We shall examine the relation of both these kinds of semantic variable to concept formation.

Finally, there are the syntactic properties of language to relate to the logical structure of thought. Hitherto, the cross-cultural study of the relation between syntax and thought has been sorely neglected, although D. McNeill (1965) suggests that there is reason to believe that the lexical encoding of events is but a special (and perhaps trivial) case of grammatical encoding. Sapir (1921) may have been the earliest to think explicitly and clearly about the manner in which syntax can shape thought.

In the view of linguistic relativity inspired by Whorf, language is seen as a system of related categories that both incorporates and perpetuates a particular world view. On the lexical level, every language codes certain domains of experience in more detail than others. It has been suggested that when a given language symbolizes a phenomenon in a single word, it is readily available as a classifying principle to speakers of that language. Although any familiar experience can be coded in any language through the simple expedient of a paraphrase, experiences that *must* be expressed in this way are supposed to be less available to speakers of the language (Brown, 1958). Some experiments have focused on this sort of difference between languages. Others have focused on the fact that grammatical considerations force certain classificatory dimensions on speakers of a given language (for example, time for speakers of English, shape for speakers of Navaho) and derive the hypothesis that the dimensions thus emphasized should be more available for cognitive use in categorization, discrimination, and so forth, to speakers of that language than for speakers of another language without such obligatory distinctions.

Why have experiments generated by these ideas yielded such diverse and confusing results? Under what conditions (if any) can a relatively rich or poor lexicon defined only by *number* of terms affect nonlinguistic cognitive activity?

Hypotheses about the effect of "numerical richness" can be based on a comparison of different languages with respect to the same domain or a comparison of different areas within a single language. Research has for the most part yielded ambiguous or negative results for studies of the first kind (interlingual), while a good number of the intralingual studies have confirmed the "richness" hypothesis. A close look reveals, however, that these two types of research differ in other ways than their results. The intracultural studies have used as their cognitive measure some memory task such as recognition of the identity of denoted stimuli earlier encountered. One classic experiment, done by Brown and Lenneberg (1954), showed, for example, that ease in *naming* colors made recognizing them easier when they appeared in a larger array. The cross-cultural studies, on the other hand, have usually dealt with judgments of *similarity* among *several* stimuli rather than with the *identity* of a *single* stimulus over time. A classic experiment was done by Carroll and Casagrande (1958), in which children were asked which of two stimuli (for example, a yellow block and a blue rope) would go best with a third item which was like one of the pair in color and like the other in shape. The subjects were Navaho-dominant and English-dominant Navaho children and white children from three to ten years of age. The Navaho-dominant children were expected to be more sensitive to form than the other groups, because Navaho has an obligatory distinction in its verbs: the *form* of an object dictates the verb of handling. The Navaho-dominant Indian children did indeed classify by form more frequently than did the English-dominant ones, but, alas, the white children who knew *no* Navaho used form most frequently of all! Other experiments have found much the same kind of anomaly (for example, Doob, 1960; Maclay, 1958).

McNeill (1965), in reviewing this literature, concludes that language does not influence perception but only memory. He proposes that a perceptual representation consists of both a schema—the linguistic label—and a correction—the visual image; but with time the correction and its label tend to be lost, thus accounting for the influence of language on memory.[1] The implication is that the cross-cultural studies mentioned above were unsuccessful because they dealt with present perceptual processes. Indeed, the one unambiguously successful cross-cultural study (Lenneberg and Roberts, 1956) involved a memory task. Before evaluating this formulation, consider the following experiment (Bruner, et al., 1966): Children were presented with pictures in sets of three. They were asked to choose the two out of each three that were not alike and to give a reason for their choice. In each of the triads, two pictures were similar in color, two were similar in form, and two were similar in the function of the object pictured. French or Wolof was the language of the subjects who took part in the experiment in a manner presently to be related.

But consider first the Wolof and French lexicons available for dealing with the task. Only words at a single level of generality—the most specific—will be considered at this point. In Wolof, it is impossible to make explicit the three color groupings possible in the experiment without the supplementary aid of French words. Specifically, in the last set of three pictures, the French word *bleu* (blue) must be used if one is to specify the basis of grouping by naming the color, for there is no single word for this color in Wolof. In the second set, color-grouping involves contrasting a pair of predominantly orange pictures with a predominantly red one. The Wolof language codes both colors with a single word (*honka*), so that verbalizing the basis of the grouping by means of the Wolof word

[1] The expression "tend to get lost" is advisable, for it is sometimes the case that the correction is not lost but magnified, producing exaggeration in memory—the familiar opposition between "leveling" and "sharpening" introduced long ago by Bartlett (1932) and the Gestalt theorists (for example, Koffka, 1935).

could not be as satisfactory as using the French word *orange*, for it would not contrast the pair with the third member of the set. For the first set of three pictures, Wolof does almost as well with coding the relevant colors as French, although yellow, the color involved in forming the color pair, is not as codable by Wolof according to the criterion (suggested by Brown, 1958) of agreement between speakers of the language. In fact, the same word is sometimes used to name both yellow and orange, the "contrasting" color of the third picture in the triad.

Let us pass over a comparison of the coding of shapes by the French and Wolof languages, for the relative strength of the two languages is much less clear, and this comparison is not necessary for present purposes. With regard to functional grouping, both easily find ways of saying, "These things are to eat, to wear, to ride in." One cannot say that Wolof is superior to French in this regard, but unlike the color case, it is not clearly inferior in its ability to code at least those aspects of function demanded by the functional groups in this experiment.

On lexical grounds, then, one would at very least expect that monolingual Wolofs would be less color-oriented and more functionally oriented in the content of their groupings than bilinguals, and that both of these groups would form fewer color and more functional groups than monolingual French children, in a forced-choice situation, where one type of attribute must be used at the expense of others.

The results, however, were unambiguously contrary to these expectations. The Wolof monolinguals, that is, the unschooled bush Wolofs, could use nothing but color as a grouping principle even when given a chance to make second choice groupings. The other groups of children, in sharp contrast, used color less and less with age and increasingly turned to the other types of attribute. Obviously, the lack of color words does *not* stop monolingual Wolofs from grouping by color.

But does it make their color discriminations less accurate? In asking this question, our experiment becomes in one respect like the intracultural tests of the Whorfian hypothesis described above; the task now involves the accuracy of color discriminations. It is no longer a matter of choice between color or form as bases of grouping. It is quite a straightforward matter to identify errors in color discrimination that can be directly related to lexical structuring. For example, the second set of pictures consists of two predominantly orange pictures and one predominantly red one. The orange colors are in fact identical. An error was counted when a child who claimed to be grouping according to color would select one orange and one red picture as being *most* similar. This choice was clearly wrong from an objective point of view, for he could have chosen the two orange ones that were of identical color. If such errors of discrimination are due to lexical coding. Wolof monolinguals should make them most frequently, Wolof bilinguals next most frequently, and French monolinguals not at all. The results are exactly as predicted. At every age, bilinguals make fewer errors of this kind than Wolof monolinguals, and the French bilingual children make no such errors at all.

These errors, by absolute standards, are infrequent, even in those groups of children where they occur most often. There are never more than three color discrimination errors in any single group (comprising about twenty children). These relatively rare mistakes are not a major conceptual feature in the total context of Wolof equivalence grouping. We begin to wonder whether the lexical features of language should be assigned as large a role in thought as has been claimed by Whorf and even others who have spoken of covariation rather than determinism.

Of great theoretical interest is the fact that these perceptual errors decrease with age until at last they are completely eliminated in all groups. It appears that age brings increasingly accurate perceptual discriminations. This would appear to be a universal trend, even when the lexicon of a culture hinders rather than facilitates such discrimination. One may conclude that with age the constraints of reality increasingly overcome language if they are opposed.

Is it, as McNeill (personal communication, 1966) suggests, that such findings prove merely that people learn to see? Clearly language influences perception and not just memory, at least during childhood. As early as 1915, Peters (cited in Smith, 1943) experimentally produced color matching errors in children through teaching them an artificial vocabulary in which certain colors were lexically indistinguishable. Later, when the children were taught these lexical distinctions, the corresponding perceptual discriminations also appeared. Even earlier, Tucker (1911) observed this same situation naturally and intraculturally; he found that children would group together different colored wools called by the same name. Lenneberg, on the other hand, confirms the notion that this influence of lexicon on perception diminishes with age; for he finds that the absence of certain terminological color distinctions adversely affects color memory in Zuni adults (Lenneberg and Roberts, 1956) and present color perception in Wolof *children* but does not affect present perception in Zuni adults (Lenneberg, 1961). Even adults, however, may fall back on language to aid perception when conditions become particularly difficult, as, for example, when all the relevant stimuli are present but spatially separated (Bruner, Postman and Rodrigues, 1951). Indeed, in terms of the eye movements necessary to visual perception, spatial separation may be translated into a mild form of temporal separation.

McNeill's hypothesis about language affecting only the memory pattern is plainly false. Yet his notions of schema plus correction may still hold. In fact, Ranken (1963) shows that *linguistic coding* in the form of assigning names can help when it is a matter of ordering shapes relative to one another *where it is not necessary to remember their exact form,* but that is can hinder performance in tasks where the precise image of the same stimuli must be utilized (as in a mental jigsaw puzzle). This outcome is interpreted to mean that the label helps where a general schema suffices for the cognitive task in question, but that it produces deceptive vagueness where the task actually involves both schema and correction, that is, an exact image.

A schema can operate *only* when called into play; language affects cognition *only* if a linguistic coding occurs, that is, only if the stimulus is given a verbal representation. It is possible that these conditions prevail only when a task is difficult to perform by means *other* than linguistic coding. But that is a moot point much in need of further investigation. Perhaps, too, different cultures vary in their tendency to use such linguistic encoding. Unschooled Wolof children in the present experiment, for instance, showed a much stronger tendency to use ostensive, as opposed to verbal, reasons for their groupings. That is, they would "explain" their grouping choice by pointing to the common pictorial elements. Such ostensive definition may have counteracted the detrimental effects of an inexact vocabulary by bypassing language altogether. We do well to remember, in assessing cross-cultural studies, that most cultures are nontechnically traditional, less verbally oriented than our own.

In summary, it appears from this and other work that linguistic encoding of the stimuli relevant to a given problem situation can affect the ordering of stimuli by providing a formula for relating them across time (Brown and Lenneberg, 1954; Van de Geer and Frijda, 1961; Lantz, 1963; Lantz and Stefflre, 1964; Koen, 1965) or space, as our Wolof results and the Bruner, Postman, and Rodrigues (1951) experiments show. The influence of encoding becomes stronger as cognitive conditions become more difficult, making an ikonic approach to the problem increasingly ineffective and a symbolic approach more crucial. Such conditions are produced as the situation becomes less "simultaneous" and more a matter of memory and as the number of stimuli to be dealt with simultaneously approaches 7 ± 2, the limit of immediate perception and memory (Miller, 1956; Brown and Lenneberg, 1954). These generalizations about the conditions under which linguistic encoding will affect other cognitive operations must be further qualified. They hold only if a linguistic representation is available to the person in question and has been activated.

Whether or not the linguistic effect will be positive or negative depends on the fit between linguistic representation and situation. If linguistic encoding is *inappropriate* to the task at hand, either because the labels do not encode all the necessary information (the mental jigsaw puzzle in Ranken's experiment), or because the labels cut the domain in places other than those the task demands, linguistic organization can have an adverse affect on task performance (for example, Lenneberg and Roberts, 1956). Whether or not a label encodes all the necessary information depends not only on the task but also on the array of stimuli. A given label becomes ineffective in distinguishing a given stimulus if it must be discriminated from others to which the name could also apply (Lantz and Stefflre, 1964).

We began by considering the part that a lexicon plays in determining the content of equivalence groupings. We have emerged with the conclusion that factors other than lexicon determine the bases or dimensions of equivalence but that a specific lexicon may influence the "band width" of the individual categories that constitute the dimension. In the end, we have seen that the equivalence of two spatially separated stimuli is affected similarly by lexical conditions as that of two temporally separated stimuli. Thus, "equivalence" and recognition have much in common.

Let us turn now from the role of labels per se to the role of a set of hierarchically organized labels, that is, to the role of lexical richness defined in structural terms. There has been much controversy about the role of superordinate words in conceptual thought. The Wolof language, in contrast to French (and to English), has neither the word "color" nor the word "shape." It is clear from the results reported above that the lack of the word "color" does not hinder color groupings from being formed. Does the absence of the general word, however, mean that the Wolofs have no general concept of color? If not, is there much consequence in this seemingly grievous deficit?

Here is one possible representation of the hierarchical structure of the first set of three pictures used in the present experiment:

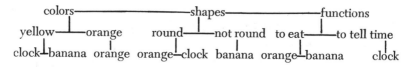

If this hierarchical organization corresponds to the type of structure generated by the subject to deal with the task, then his use of the superordinate words "color" or "shape" should indicate that the person is operating at the top of the hierarchy and has access to the entire hierarchy. One would predict, then, that he would be able to supply more than one kind of attribute if pressed. For he is plainly contrasting, say, *color* with *shape* or with *use*. By the same reasoning, his exclusive use of shape names or color names alone (for example, "round," "yellow") would mean that he was operating one level lower in the hierarchy. He would be "cut off" from the top of the hierarchy and its connections with other branches. He would therefore be less likely to operate in branches other than the one in which he found himself. A concept (a consciously or explicitly recognized concept) is defined as much by what it excludes as by what it includes, by its contrast class. The concept of color per se comes into being through contrast with an opposing idea. An opposing concept to color per se cannot be a specific color: just as "round" is related only to other shapes, so "yellow" relates only to other colors.

If this reasoning is correct, then one would expect that, if a subject ever used an abstract word like "color" or "shape," he would also vary his choice of grouping attributes when asked to make a first and second choice of pairs for each of the three sets of pictures. But if he used only a concrete word like "red," then one would expect him to form nothing but color groupings in all six tasks. Our results do indeed indicate that there is a significant association between use of superordinate words like "color" and "shape" and the number of different types of attribute used for grouping. And this relationship holds when all other factors such as knowledge of French and school grade are held constant. Thus, if a Wolof child uses a superordinate word, his chances of grouping by a variety of attributes are twice as great as those of a child who utilizes no superordinate vocabulary. Recall that when a Wolof child uses the word "color," it is a French word that he is introducing into a Wolof linguistic context.

Although all the present experimentation was carried out in Wolof, additional sixth grade Wolof groups in French were used in order to assess the effect of using one language or another when all other factors are held constant. The relationship between use of superordinate words and variety of attribute used is weakest under this condition. But before interpreting this finding, consider one further observation. The experiment was also carried out in French with French children in the sixth grade. It is in this experiment that the strongest relationship is found. If a French child uses an abstract "top-of-the-hierarchy" label, he is almost certain to vary his basis of grouping at least once. So we must conclude that access to the pure conceptual hierarchy as diagrammed is indicated by the use of abstract terms *only if* the linguistic terms have been thoroughly mastered in all their semantic implications. The results indicate that such is the case under normal conditions of spontaneous use in the context of one's native language. But when the Wolof children are interrogated in French, their use of superordinate language seems to have a forced character and indicates little about hierarchical structure and where they are in that structure.

The reasons for color preference among the Wolof are too complicated to discuss here. What needs emphasis is that the basis of equivalence is not an either/or phenomenon, as so much experimentation has assumed. It is, rather, a matter of adding new bases to old and of *integrating them in a hier-archically organized structure.* Everybody is more or less limited in the range of classificatory bases available to him. It is not that one person uses color, the other shape. Rather, one can use color, the other can use shape *and* color. It is the structure of the lexicon and not simply its list of terms that is crucial.

Superordinate class words are not just a luxury for people who do not have to deal with concrete phenomena, as Roger Brown (1958) hypothesizes. In a way quite different from that envisaged by Whorf in the lexical version of his hypothesis, we seem to have found an important correspondence between linguistic and conceptual structure. But it relates not to words in isolation but to their depth of hierarchical embedding both in the language and in thought. This correspondence has to do not with quantitative richness of vocabulary in different domains or with "accessibility" but with the presence or absence of higher order words that can be used to integrate different domains of words and objects into hierarchical structures. No matter how rich the vocabulary available to describe a given domain, it is of limited use as an instrument of thought if it is not organized into a hierarchy that can be activated as a whole.

Consider now the grammatical aspect of language. In previous work (Vygotsky, 1961; Bruner, et al., 1966) the structure of equivalence groupings was found to become increasingly superordinate with age and less complexive and thematic. Superordinate structure is not the same as the use of a general or superordinate word. The attribute that organizes a superordinate group may be general or specific, but it must be explicitly stated to be shared by every member of the group in question. Thus, "they are all the same color" would have the same structural status as "they are all red." In terms of this structural criterion, all the children studied in Senegal conform to the usual development trend. Although the grouping *choices* of the unschooled Wolof group got increasingly systematic with age, their explanations showed a somewhat different form. Instead of explicitly connecting the common attribute to every member of their groupings in the manner described above, they would explain their grouping with a single word, saying, for example, nothing more than "red." What may we make of this?

Consider the matter in purely grammatical terms. For perhaps we can find a connection between conceptual organization and grammatical rules. Let us posit, first, three stages of symbolic reference. The first is the ostensive mode: mere pointing at the object of reference. The second, the labeling mode, consists of nothing more than a verbal tag. This tag replaces or accompanies the operation of pointing. The third mode is sentential. Here the label is integrated into a complete sentence. In the present experiment, these three modes were defined as follows, and the definitions applied to grouping reasons: (1) pointing—no verbal response; (2) labeling—label only; no *verb* in utterance, for example, "red"; (3) sentential placement—complete sentence, for example, "this is red."

Among French monolinguals, pointing is nonexistent even among first graders. Pointing, however, occupies a definite position in the reasoning of all the youngest Wolof groups, especially the unschooled, but disappears in all the groups with advancing age. The other differences set the unschooled children apart from all the school children. In the unschooled groups, labeling, the simple paradigmatic mode, increases with age. But the use of sentential placement does not increase with age but remains at a constantly low level. In all the school groups, both Wolof-French bilingual and French monolingual, the ostensive mode gives way to sentential placement with age and increased schooling. There is, let it be noted, virtually no difference on any criterion between the oldest French mono-linguals and the oldest Wolof-French bilinguals *when the experiment is run in French.* The superiority is slightly on the side of the French when the experiment is carried out in the native language of each group. The contrast that is most dramatic is between Wolof children in school speaking French and those not in school speaking Wolof, with virtually no over-lap in the distributions. Some 97 per cent of the eleven- to thirteen-year-old Wolof monolinguals (the unschooled Wolof children) use the labeling mode; 90 per cent of the Wolof sixth graders doing the experiment in French use the sentential mode.

These results using grammatical criteria reveal larger differ-ences between the groups who know French and those who do not than those using the earlier, more semantic verbal measure of grouping structure. Is there, however, any direct relation between grammatical and conceptual structure? A child can frame an explicit superordinate structure in either the labeling or sentential modes. This superordinate structure can be of a general or itemized type. An example of a general superordinate language structure in the labeling mode would be "These—round." Expressed sententially, the structure would be "These (or "They") are round." An itemized superordinate in labeling form might be "This—round; this—round." An ex-ample of the same structure expressed in the sentential mode would be "This (or "It") is round; this (or "it") is round." Obviously, a limitless variety of nonsuperordinate structures may be expressed either as labels or as complete sentences. It is valid, then, to ask whether the use of a particular mode of reference is associated with a particular conceptual structure. The answer is a strong affirmative for both schooled and unschooled Wolof children. When a school child frames a reason in the sentential mode, the probability that he will form a superordinate structure of either the itemized or general type is on the average almost three times as great as when he uses simple labeling. For an unschooled child, this same probability of a superordinate structure is almost six times as great when his reasons are sentences rather than labels.

For a school child, moreover, the probability that a superordinate structure will be in a general (rather than itemized) form is more than four times as great when a grouping reason is expressed in the sentential mode. In the unschooled groups, the number of reasons falling into these categories is very small. If, however, all four unschooled groups are combined, the relationship does hold: superordinate reasons expressed as labels take the general form about half as often as do those expressed as complete sentences.

We are led to the hypothesis that school is operating on grouping operations through the training embodied in the written language. This hypothesis has a good theoretical basis. The written language, as Vygotsky (1961) points out, provides an occasion in which one must deploy language out of the immediate context of reference. Writing virtually forces a remoteness of reference on the language user. Consequently, he cannot use simple pointing as an aid, nor can he count on labeling that depends on the present context to make clear what his label refers to. Writing, then, is training in the use of linguistic contexts that are independent of the immediate referents. Thus, the embedding of a label in a sentence structure indicates that it is less tied to its situational context and more related to its linguistic context. The implications of this fact for manipulability are great; linguistic contexts can be turned upside down more easily than real ones can. Indeed, the linguistic independence of context achieved by certain grammatical modes appears to favor the development of the more self-contained superordinate structure used by the school children.

Note the recurrence of a theme that has been running through all of our results: it is always the schooling variable that makes qualitative differences in directions of growth.

Wolof children who have been to school are more different intellectually from unschooled children living in the same bush village than they are from city children in the same country or from Mexico City, Anchorage, Alaska or Brookline, Massachusetts (Bruner, et al., 1966). Similar results demonstrating the huge impact of school have emerged from the Belgian Congo (Cryns, 1962) and South Africa (Biesheuvel, 1949; and personal communication from W. H. O. Schmidt, 1965).

How, then, do school and language interrelate? We may hypothesize that it is the fact of being a *written* language that makes French such a powerful factor in the cognitive growth of the children we have studied. For all of the semantic and syntactic features that we have discussed in relation to concept formation—a rich vocabulary that is hierarchically organized, syntactical embedding of labels, etc.—become necessary when one must communicate *out of the context* of immediate reference. And it is precisely in this respect that written language differs from spoken. But school itself provides the same opportunity to use language out of context—even spoken language—for, to a very high degree, what one talks about are things not immediately present.

SCHOOL, LANGUAGE, AND INDIVIDUALISM

In the last section, the final emphasis was on the role of school in establishing context-independent modes of thinking through the separation of the written word from the thing it stands for and the separation of school from life. How exactly does this process relate to the decline of a "realistic" world view and the correlative rise in self-consciousness discussed in the section before? Realism, as a world view, can characterize a person's concept of language and words, as well as his concept of thought in general. When a word is considered to be as "real" as the thing for which it stands, the psychological attitude (and philosophical position) is called nominal or verbal realism. School separates word and thing and destroys verbal realism by presenting for the first time a situation where words are systematically and continually "there" without their referents. The rules of the "Original Word Game" described by Brown (1958), in which the tutor acts as though things are but signs of their names, are for the first time systematically and thoroughly broken. That is, the sequence object-name no longer is invariant. When names, or symbols in general, no longer inhere in their referents, they must go somewhere; and the logical place is the psyche of the language user. Thus, the separation of word and thing demands a notion that words are in people's heads, not in their referents. (This point has been well made by Ogden and Richards, 1930.) The concepts "thinker" and "thought processes" thus become important in the shedding of nominal realism. Meaning is seen to vary with the particular speaker, and the notion of psychological relativity is born. Implicit in this notion is the distinctness of oneself and one's own point of view. Thus, the individual must conceptually separate himself from the group; he must become self-conscious, aware of having a particular slant on things, a certain individuality.

The destruction of nominal or verbal realism may thus be the wedge that ultimately fragments the unitary solidarity of a "realistic" world view. Once thought has been dissociated from its objects, the stage is set for symbolic processes to run ahead of concrete fact, for thought to be in terms of possibility rather than actuality. At this point, symbolic representation can go beyond the capacities of an ikonic system (Bruner, 1964), and the way is open for Piaget's stage of formal operations, where the real becomes but a subset of the possible (Inhelder and Piaget, 1958). So school and the written language may have a privileged position in the shift from a collective to an individualistic orientation chronicled above.

CULTURE AND BIOLOGICAL GROWTH

Lest the foregoing seem to support a view of complete cultural determinism, which it does not, some remarks on the interaction of cultural constraints and universal biological maturation seem appropriate in conclusion.

Because the doctrine that ontogeny recapitulates phylogeny

was given too literal a form in biology, a more sophisticated consideration of the relation between phylogeny and ontogeny was also given up. Species-specific behavior does not appear out of the blue. It has evolutionary history, and that history reflects itself in the early growth of the young. We are primates, and our primate heritage affects our growth. All cultures must work on the stuff of the biological organism, specifically on man's primate constraints.

One of the huge discontinuities in man's evolution was his capacity for language and symbolism, and this only gradually achieves realization through training. Sapir (1921) may have been quite right in pointing out that no human language can be shown to be more sophisticated than any other and that the speech used by the member of the Academy is no more complex than that of a Hottentot. But again it was Sapir who pointed out that it is in extracting from our use of language the powerful tools for organizing thought that peoples differ from each other. The intellectual nurturing that makes it possible eventually to use language as a tool of thought requires long years and complex training.

It is here that the difference comes. If that intellectual training is not forthcoming, if language is not freely employed in its pragmatic function of guiding thought and action, then one finds forms of intellectual functioning that are adequate for concrete tasks but not so for matters involving abstract conception. As Werner (1948) pointed out, "Development among primitive people is characterized on the one hand by precocity and, on the other, by a relatively early arrest of the process of intellectual growth." His remark is telling with respect to the difference we find between school children and those who have not been to school. The latter stabilize earlier and do not go on to new levels of operation. The same "early arrest" characterizes the differences between "culturally-deprived" and other American children (for example, Deutsch, 1965).

In short, some environments "push" cognitive growth better, earlier, and longer than others. What does not seem to happen is that different cultures produce completely divergent and unrelated modes of thought. The reason for this must be the constraint of our biological heritage.[2] That heritage makes it possible for man to reach a form of intellectual maturity that is capable of elaborating a highly technical society. Less demanding societies—less demanding intellectually—do not produce as much symbolic embedding and elaboration of first ways of looking and thinking. Whether one wishes to "judge" these differences on some universal human scale as favoring an intellectually more evolved man is a matter of one's values. But however one judges, let it be clear that a decision *not* to aid the intellectual maturation of those who live in less technically developed societies can not be premised on the careless claim that it makes little difference.

[2] This constraint is, however, somewhat variable in that widespread malnutrition can affect the neurological and mental functions of large groups of people (Biesheuvel, 1943, 1949, 1956, 1963).

3

The Growth
of Mind

What is most unique about man is that his growth as an individual depends upon the history of his species—not upon a history reflected in genes and chromosomes but, rather, reflected in a culture external to man's tissue and wider in scope than is embodied in any one man's competency. Perforce, then, the growth of mind is always growth assisted from the outside. And since a culture, particularly an advanced one, transcends the bounds of individual competence, the limits for individual growth are by definition greater than what any single person has previously attained. For the limits of growth depend on how a culture assists the individual to use such intellectual potential as he may possess.

AMPLIFYING SKILLS AND KNOWLEDGE

What a culture does to assist the development of the powers of mind of its members is, in effect, to provide amplification systems to which human beings, equipped with appropriate skills, can link themselves. There are, first, the amplifiers of action—hammers, levers, digging sticks, wheels—but more important, the programs of action into which such implements can be substituted. Second, there are amplifiers of the senses, ways of looking and noticing that can take advantage of devices ranging from smoke signals and hailers to diagrams and pictures that stop the action or microscopes that enlarge it. Finally and most powerfully, there are amplifiers of the thought processes, ways of thinking that employ language and formation of explanation, and later use such languages as mathematics and logic and even find automatic servants to crank out the consequences. A culture is, then, a deviser, a repository, and a transmitter of amplification systems and of the devices that fit into such systems.

But it is reasonably clear that there is a major difference between the mode of transmission in a technical society, with its schools, and an indigenous one, where cultural transmission is in the context of action. It is not just that an indigenous society, when its action pattern becomes disrupted, falls apart—at a most terrifying rate—as in uncontrolled urbanization in some parts of Africa. Rather, it is that the institution of a school serves to convert knowledge and skill into more symbolical, more abstract, more verbal form. It is this process of transmission—admittedly very new in human history—that is so poorly understood and to which, finally, we shall return.

There are certain obvious specifications that can be stated about how a society must proceed in order to equip its young. It must convert what is to be known—whether a skill or a belief system or a connected body of knowledge—into a form capable of being mastered by a beginner. The more we know of the process of growth, the better we shall be at such conversion. The failure of modern man to understand mathematics and science may be less a matter of stunted abilities than our failure to understand how to teach such subjects. Second, given the limited amount of time available for learning, there must be a due regard for saving the learner from needless learning. There must be some emphasis placed on economy and transfer and the learning of general rules. All societies must (and virtually all do) distinguish those who are clever from those who are stupid—though few of them generalize this trait across all activities. Cleverness in a particular activity almost universally connotes strategy, economy, heuristics, highly generalized skills. A society must also place emphasis upon how one derives a course of action from what one has learned. Indeed, in an indigenous society it is almost impossible to separate what one does from what one knows. More advanced societies often have not found a way of dealing with the separation of knowledge and action—probably a result of the emphasis they place upon "telling" in their instruction. All societies must maintain interest among the young in the learning process, a minor problem when learning is in the context of life and action, but harder when it becomes more abstracted. Once these matters are in hand, a society assures that its necessary skills and procedures remain intact from one generation to the next—which does not always happen, as witnessed by Easter Islanders, Incas, Aztecs, and Mayas.[1]

Psychologists have too easily assumed that learning is learning is learning—that the early version of what was taught did not matter much, one thing being much like another and reducible to a pattern of association, to stimulus-response connections, or to our favorite molecular componentry. We denied there was a problem of development beyond the quantitative

[1] I have purposely left out of the discussion the problems of impulse regulation and socialization of motives, topics that have received extended treatment in the voluminous literature on culture and personality. The omission is dictated by emphasis rather than evaluation. Obviously, the shaping of character by culture is of great importance for an understanding of our topic as it bears, for example, upon culture-instilled attitudes toward the uses of mind. Since the psychologist's emphasis is upon human potential and its amplification by culturally patterned instrumental skills, I mention the problem of character formation in passing and in recognition of its importance in a complete treatment of the issues under discussion.

one of providing more experience, and with a denial, closed our eyes to the pedagogical problem of how to represent knowledge, how to sequence it, how to embody it in a form appropriate to young learners. We expended more passion on the part-whole controversy than on what whole or what part of it was to be presented first. I should except Piaget (1954), Köhler (1940), and Vygotsky (1962) from these complaints— all until recently unheeded voices.

The psychologist's neglect of the economy of learning stems, ironically, from the heritage of Ebbinghaus (1913), who was vastly interested in savings. Nonsense syllables, random mazes failed to take into account how we reduce complexity and strangeness to simplicity and the familiar, how we convert what we have learned into rules and procedures, how, to use Bartlett's (1932) term of over thirty years ago, we turn around on our own schemata to reorganize what we have mastered into more manageable form.

Nor have psychologists taken naturally to the issue of knowledge and action. Its apparent mentalism has repelled us. Tolman (1951), who bravely made the distinction, was accused of leaving his organisms wrapt in thought. But he recognized the problem and if he insisted on the idea that knowledge might be organized in cognitive maps, it was in recognition (as a great functionalist) that organisms go somewhere on the basis of what they have learned. I believe we are getting closer to the problem of how knowledge affects action and vice versa, and offer in testimony of my conviction the provocative book by Miller, Galanter, and Pribram (1960), *Plans and the Structure of Behavior.*

Where the maintenance of the learner's interest is concerned, I emphasize what my colleague Gordon Allport (1946) had long warned. We have been so concerned with the model of driven behavior, with drive reduction and the *vis a tergo* that, again, until recently, we have tended to overlook the question of what keeps learners interested in the activity of learning, in the achievement of competence beyond bare necessity and first payoff. The work of R. W. White (1959) on effectance motivation, of Harlow and his colleagues (Butler, 1954; Harlow, 1953) on curiosity, and of Heider (1958) and Festinger (1962) on consistency begins to redress the balance. But it is only a beginning.

I have tried to examine briefly what a culture must do in passing on its amplifying skills and knowledge to a new generation and, even more briefly, how psychologists have dealt or failed to deal with the problems. I think the situation is fast changing—with a sharp increase in interest in the conversion problem, the problems of economy of learning, the nature of interest, the relation of knowledge and action. We are, I believe, at a major turning point where psychology will once again concern itself with the design of methods of assisting cognitive growth, be it through the invention of a rational technology of toys, of ways of enriching the environment of the crib and nursery, of organizing the activity of a school, or of devising a curriculum whereby we transmit an organized body of knowledge and skill to a new generation to amplify their powers of mind.

CONSTRUCTING A COURSE OF STUDY

There is strikingly little knowledge available about the "third way" of training the skills of the young: the first being the play practice of component skills in prehuman primates, the second the teaching-in-context of indigenous societies, and the third being the abstracted, detached method of the school.

Let me now become highly specific. Let me consider a particular course of study, one given in a school of the kind that exists in Western culture. My and my colleagues' experience in constructing an upper elementary social sciences course, "Man: A Course of Study (1965)", may serve to highlight the kinds of problems and conjectures one encounters in studying how to assist the growth of intellect in this "third way." The "we" I employ in this context is no editorial fiction but rather a group of anthropologists, zoologists, linguists, theoretical engineers, artists, designers, camera crews, teachers, children, and psychologists. The project was carried out at the Education Development Center (formerly Educational Services, Incorporated), with grants from the National Science Foundation and the Ford Foundation.

There is a dilemma in describing a course of study. One begins by setting forth the intellectual substance of what is to be taught. Yet if such a recounting tempts one to "get across" the subject, the ingredient of pedagogy is in jeopardy. For only in a trivial sense is a course designed to "get something across," merely to impart information. There are better means to that end than teaching. Unless the learner develops his skills, disciplines his taste, deepens his view of the world, the "something" that is got across is hardly worth the effort of transmission.

The more "elementary" a course and the younger its students, the more serious must be its pedagogical aim of forming the intellectual powers of those whom it serves. It is as important to justify a good mathematics course by the intellectual discipline it provides or the honesty it promotes as by the mathematics it transmits. Indeed, neither can be accomplished without the other. The content of this particular course is man: his nature as a species, the forces that shaped and continue to shape his humanity. Three questions recur throughout: What is human about human beings? How did they get that way? How can they be made more so?

In pursuit of our questions we explore five matters, each closely associated with the evolution of man as a species, each defining at once the distinctiveness of man and his potentiality for further evolution. The five great humanizing forces are, of course, tool making, language, social organization, the management of man's prolonged childhood, and man's urge to explain. It has been our first lesson in teaching that no pupil, however eager, can appreciate the relevance of, say, tool making or language in human evolution without first grasping the fundamental concept of a tool or what a language is. These are not self-evident matters, even to the expert. So we are involved in teaching not only the role of tools or language in the emergence of man but, as a necessary precondition for doing so, setting forth the fundamentals of linguistics or the theory of tools. And it is as often the case as not that (as in the case of the "theory of tools") we must solve a formidable intellectual problem ourselves in order to be able to help our pupils do the same.

While one readily singles out five sources of man's humanization, under no circumstances can they be put into airtight compartments. Human kinship is distinctively different from primate mating patterns precisely because it is classificatory and rests on man's ability to use language. Or, if you will, tool use enhances the division of labor in a society which in turn affects kinship. So while each domain can be treated as a separate set of ideas, their teaching must make it possible for the children to have a sense of their interaction. We have leaned heavily on the use of contrast, highly controlled contrast, to help children achieve detachment from the all too familiar matrix of social life: the contrasts of man versus higher primates, contemporary technological man versus "primitive" man, and man versus child. The primates are principally baboons, and the "primitive" peoples mostly the Netsilik Eskimos of Pelly Bay. The materials collected for our purposes are on film, in story, in ethnography, in pictures and drawings, and principally in ideas embodied in exercises.

We had high aspirations. We hoped to achieve five goals:

1. To give our pupils respect for and confidence in the powers of their own minds.
2. To give them respect, moreover, for the powers of thought concerning the human condition, man's plight, and his social life.
3. To provide them with a set of workable models that make it simpler to analyze the nature of the social world in which they live and the condition in which man finds himself.
4. To impart a sense of respect for the capacities and plight of man as a species, for his origins, for his potential, for his humanity.
5. To leave the student with a sense of the unfinished business of man's evolution.

One last word about the course of study that has to do with the quality of the ideas, materials, and artistry—a matter that is at once technological and intellectual. We felt that the making of such a curriculum deserved the best talent and technique available in the world. Whether artist, ethnographer, film maker, poet, teacher—nobody we asked refused us.

THE PSYCHOLOGY OF A SUBJECT MATTER

Let me now try to describe some of the major problems one encounters in trying to construct a course of study. I shall not try to translate the problems into refined theoretical form, for they do not as yet merit such translation. They are more difficulties than problems. I choose them because they are vividly typical of what one encounters in such enterprises.

One special point about these difficulties. They are born of trying to achieve an objective and are as much policy bound as theory bound. It is like the difference between building an economic theory about monopolistic practices and constructing policies for controlling monopoly. Let me remind you that modern economic theory has been reformulated, refined, and revived by having a season in policy. I am convinced that the psychology of assisted growth—that is, pedagogy—will have to be forged in the policy crucible of curriculum making before it can reach its full descriptive power as theory. Economics was first through the cycle from theory to policy to theory to policy; it is happening now to psychology, anthropology, and sociology.

Now on to the difficulties. The first is what might be called *the psychology of a subject matter*. A learned discipline can be conceived as a way of thinking about certain phenomena. Mathematics is one way of thinking about order without reference to what is being ordered. The behavioral sciences provide one or perhaps several ways of thinking about man and his society—about regularities, origins, causes, effects. They are probably special (and suspect) because they permit man to look at himself from a perspective that is outside his own skin and beyond his own preferences—at least for awhile.

Underlying a discipline's "way of thought," there is a set of connected, varyingly implicit, generative propositions. In physics and mathematics, most of the underlying generative propositions like the conservation theorems, or the axioms of geometry, or the associative, distributive, and commutative rules of analysis are by now very explicit indeed. In the behavioral sciences we must be content with more implicitness. We traffic in inductive propositions: for example, the different activities of a society are interconnected such that if you know something about the technological response of a society to an environment, you will be able to make some shrewd guesses about its myths or about the things it values, etc. We use the device of a significant contrast—as when, in linguistics, we describe the restricting tradition of a baboon troop to always stay within a given range—in order to help us recognize the system of reciprocal exchange of a human group, the former somehow provoking awareness of the. latter.

There is nothing more central to a discipline than its way of thinking. There is nothing more important in its teaching than to provide the child the earliest opportunity to learn that way of thinking—the forms of connection, the attitudes, hopes, jokes, and frustrations that go with it. In a word, the best introduction to a subject is the subject itself. At the very first breath, the young learner should, we think, be given the chance to solve problems, to conjecture, to quarrel as these are done at the heart of the discipline. But, you will ask, how can this be arranged?

Here again the problem of conversion. There exist ways of thinking characteristic of different stages of development. We are acquainted with Inhelder and Piaget's (1958) account of the transition from preoperational, through concrete operational, to propositional thought in the years from preschool through, say, high school. If you have an eventual pedagogical objective in mind, you can translate the way of thought of a discipline into its Piagetian (or other) equivalent appropriate to a given level of development and take the child onward from there. The Cambridge Mathematics Project of the Education Development Center argues that if the child is to master the calculus early in his high school years, he should start work early with the idea of limits, the earliest work being manipulative, later going on to images and diagrams, and finally moving on to the more abstract notation needed for delineating the more precise idea of limits.

In "Man: A Course of Study," there are also versions of the subject appropriate to a particular age that can at a later age be given a more powerful rendering. We tried to choose topics with this in mind: The analysis of kinship that begins with children using sticks and blocks and colors and whatnot to represent their own families, goes on to the conventional kinship diagrams by a meandering but, as you can imagine, interesting path, and then can move on to more formal and powerful componential analysis. So, too, with myth. For our early tryouts, we began with the excitement of a powerful myth (like the Netsilik Nuliajik myth), then had the children construct some myths of their own, then examine what a set of Netsilik myths have in common, which takes us finally to Lévi-Strauss's (1963) analysis of contrastive features in myth construction. A variorum text of a myth or corpus of myths put together by sixth graders can be quite an extraordinary document.

This approach to the psychology of a learned discipline illuminates another problem raised earlier: the maintenance of interest. There is, in this approach, a reward in understanding that grows from the subject matter itself. It is easier to engineer this satisfaction in mathematics, for understanding is so utter in a formal discipline—a balance beam balances or it does not; therefore there is an equality or there is not. In the behavioral sciences the payoff in understanding cannot be so obviously and startlingly self-revealing. Yet, one can design exercises in the understanding of man, too—as when children figure out the ways in which, given limits of ecology, skills, and materials, Bushmen hunt different animals, and then compare their predictions with the real thing on film.

STIMULATING THOUGHT IN A SCHOOL

Consider now a second problem: *how to stimulate thought in the setting of a school.* We know from experimental studies like those of Bloom and Broder (1950), and of Goodnow and Pettigrew (1955), that there is a striking difference in the acts of a person who thinks that the task before him represents a problem to be solved rather than being controlled by random forces. School is a particular subculture where these matters are concerned. By school age, children have come to expect quite arbitrary and, from their point of view, meaningless demands to be made upon them by adults—the result, most likely, of the fact that adults often fail to recognize the task of conversion necessary to give their questions some intrinsic significance for the child. Children, of course, will try to solve problems if they recognize them as such. But they are not often either predisposed to or skillful in problem finding, in recognizing the hidden conjectural feaure in tasks set them. But we know now that children in school can quite quickly be led to such problem finding by encouragement and instruction.

The need for this instruction and encouragement and its relatively swift success relates, I suspect, to what psychoanalysts refer to as the guilt-ridden oversuppression of primary process and its public replacement by secondary process. Children, like adults, need reassurance that it is all right to entertain and express highly subjective ideas, to treat a task as a problem where you *invent* an answer rather than *finding* one out there in the book or on the blackboard. With children in elementary school, there is often a need to devise emotionally vivid special games, story-making episodes, or construction projects to reestablish in the child's mind his right not only to have his own private ideas but to express them in the public setting of a classroom.

But there is another, perhaps more serious difficulty: the interference of intrinsic problem solving by extrinsic. Young children in school expend extraordinary time and effort figuring out what it is that the teacher wants—and usually coming to the conclusion that she or he wants tidiness or remembering or doing things at a certain time in a certain way. This I refer to as extrinsic problem solving. There is a great deal of it in school.

There are several quite straightforward ways of stimulating problem solving. One is to train teachers to want it, and that will come in time. But teachers can be encouraged to like it, interestingly enough, by providing them and their children with materials and lessons that *permit* legitimate problem solving and permit the teacher to recognize it. For exercises with such materials create an atmosphere by treating things as instances of what *might* have occurred rather than simply as what did occur. Let me illustrate by a concrete instance. A fifth-grade class was working on the organization of a baboon troop—on this particular day, specifically on how they might protect against predators. They saw a brief sequence of film in which six or seven adult males go forward to intimidate and hold off three cheetahs. The teacher asked what the baboons had done to keep the cheetahs off, and there ensued a lively discussion of how the dominant adult males, by showing their formidable mouthful of teeth and making threatening gestures, had turned the trick. A boy tentatively raised his hand and asked whether cheetahs always attacked together. Yes, though a single cheetah sometimes followed behind a moving troop and picked off an older, weakened straggler or an unwary, straying juvenile. "Well, what if there were four cheetahs and two of them attacked from behind and two from in front? What would the baboons do then?" The question could have been answered empirically—and the inquiry ended. Cheetahs *do not* attack that way, and so we do not know what baboons *might* do. Fortunately, it was not. For the question opens up the deep issues of what might be and why it is not. Is there a necessary relation between predators and prey that share a common ecological niche? Must their encounters have a "sporting chance" outcome? It is such conjecture, in this case quite unanswerable, that produces rational, self-consciously problem-finding behavior so crucial to the growth of intellectual power. Given the materials, given some background and encouragement, teachers like it as much as the students.

I should like to turn now to the *personalization of knowledge*. A generation ago, the progressive movement urged that knowledge be related to the child's own experience and brought out of the realm of empty abstractions. A good idea was translated into banalities about the home, then the friendly postman and trashman, then the community, and so on. It is a poor way to compete with the child's own dramas and mysteries. Two decades ago, my colleague Clyde Kluckhohn (1949) wrote a prize-winning popular book on anthropology, with the entrancing title *Mirror for Man*. In some deep way, there is extraordinary power in "that mirror which other civilizations still hold up to us to recognize and study . . . [the] image of ourselves [Lévi-Strauss, 1965]." The psychological bases of the power are not obvious. Is it as in discrimination learning, where increasing the degree of contrast helps in the learning of a discrimination, or as in studies of concept attainment where a negative instance demonstrably defines the domain of a conceptual rule? Or is it some primitive identification? All these miss one thing that seems to come up frequently in our interviews with the children. It is the experience of discovering kinship and likeness in what at first seemed bizarre, exotic, and even a little repellant.

Consider two examples, both involving film of the Netsilik. In the films, a single nuclear family—Itimangnark, Kingnuk, and their four-year-old Umiapik—is followed through the year. Spring sealing, summer fishing at the stone weir, fall caribou hunting, early winter fishing through the ice, winter at the big ceremonial igloo. Children report that at first the three members of the family look weird and uncouth. In time they look normal, and eventually, as when Kingnuk finds sticks around which to wrap her braids, the girls speak of how pretty she is. That much is superficial—or so it seems. But consider a second episode.

It has to do with Umiapik who, with his father's help, devises a snare and catches a gull. There is a scene in which he stones the gull to death. Our children watched, horror struck. One girl, Kathy, blurted out, "He's not even human, doing that to the seagull." The class was silent. Then another girl, Jennine, said quietly: "He's got to grow up to be a hunter. His mother was smiling when he was doing that." And then an extended discussion about how people have to do things to learn and even do things to learn how to feel appropriately. "What would you do if you had to live there? Would you be as smart about getting along as they are with what they've got?" said one boy, going back to the accusation that Umiapik was inhuman to stone the bird.

I am sorry it is so difficult to say it clearly. What I am trying to say is that to personalize knowledge one does not simply link it to the familiar. Rather, one makes the familiar an instance of a more general case and thereby produces awareness of it. What the children were learning about was not seagulls and Eskimos but about their own feelings and preconceptions that, up to then, were too implicit to be recognizable to them.

Consider finally the problem of *self-conscious reflectiveness.* It is an epistemological mystery why traditional education has so often emphasized extensiveness and coverage over intensiveness and depth. We have already observed that memorizing was usually perceived by children as one of the high-priority tasks, but rarely did children sense an emphasis upon ratiocination with a view toward redefining what had been encountered, reshaping it, reordering it. The cultivation of reflectiveness, or whatever you choose to call it, is one of the great problems one faces in devising curriculum. How does one lead children to discover the powers and pleasures that await the exercise of retrospection?

Let me suggest one answer that has grown from what we have done. It is the use of the "organizing conjecture." We have used three such conjectures—what is human about human beings, how they got that way, how they could become more so. They serve two functions, one of them the very obvious though important one of putting perspective back into the particulars. The second is less obvious and considerably more surprising. The questions often seemed to serve as criteria for determining where they were getting, how well they were understanding, whether anything new was emerging. Recall Kathy's cry: "He's not human doing that to the seagull." She was hard at work in her rage on the conjecture what makes human beings human.

There, in brief, are four problems that provide some sense of what a psychologist encounters when he takes a hand in assisting the growth of mind in children in the special setting of a school. The problems look quite different from those we encounter in formulating classical developmental theory with the aid of typical laboratory research. They also look very different from those that one would find in an indigenous society, describing how children picked up skills and knowledge and values in the context of action and daily life. We clearly do not have a theory of the school that is sufficient to the task of running schools—just as we have no adequate theory of toys or of readiness building or whatever the jargon is for preparing children to do a better job the next round. It only obscures the issue to urge that some day our classical theories of learning will fill the gap. They show no sign of doing so.

I hope that psychologists will not allow themselves to be embarrassed by their present ignorance. It has been a long time since they have looked at what is involved in imparting knowledge through the vehicle of the school—if ever they did look at it squarely. Let us delay no longer.

But I am deeply convinced that the psychologist cannot alone construct a theory of how to assist cognitive development and cannot alone learn how to enrich and amplify the powers of a growing human mind. The task belongs to the whole intellectual community: the behavioral scientists and the artists, scientists, and scholars who are the custodians of skill, taste, and knowledge in our culture. The special task of psychologists is to convert skills and knowledge to forms and exercises that fit growing minds—and it is a task ranging from how to keep children free from anxiety and how to translate physics for the very young child into a set of playground maneuvers that, later, the child can turn around upon and convert into a sense of inertial regularities. Psychology is peculiarly prey to parochialism. Left to their own devices, psychologists tend to construct models of a man who is neither a victim of history, a target of economic forces, nor even a working member of a society. I am still struck by Roger Barker's (1963) ironic truism that the best way to predict the behavior of a human being is to know where he is: In a post office he behaves post office, at church he behaves church.

Psychology, and you will forgive me if the image seems a trifle frivolous, thrives on polygamy with her neighbors. Its marriage with the biological sciences has produced a cumulation of ever more powerful knowledge. So, too, its joint undertakings with anthropology and sociology. Joined together with a variety of disciplines, psychologists have made lasting contributions to the health sciences and, I judge, will make even greater contributions now that the emphasis is shifting to the problems of alleviating stress and arranging for a community's mental health. What I find lacking is an alignment that might properly be called the growth sciences. The field of pedagogy is one participant in the growth sciences. Any field of inquiry devoted to assisting the growth of effective human beings, fully empowered with zest, with skill, with knowledge, with taste is surely a candidate for this sodality. My friend Philip Morrison once suggested to his colleagues at Cornell that his department of physics grant a doctorate not only for work in theoretical, experimental, or applied physics, but also for work in pedagogical physics. The limits of the growth sciences remain to be drawn. They surely transcend the behavioral sciences cum pediatrics. It is plain that, if we are to achieve the effectiveness of which we as human beings are capable, there will one day have to be such a field.

4

Some Elements
of Discovery

I am not quite sure I understand anymore what discovery is and I don't think it matters very much. But a few things can be said about how people can be helped to discover things for themselves.

A word of caution first. You cannot consider education without taking into account how a culture gets passed on. It seems to me highly unlikely that given the centrality of culture in man's adaptation to his environment—the fact that culture serves him in the same way as changes in morphology served earlier in the evolutionary scale—that, biologically speaking, one would expect each organism to rediscover the totality of its culture—this would seem most unlikely. Moreover, it seems equally unlikely, given the nature of man's dependency as a creature, that this long period of dependency characteristic of our species was designed entirely for the most inefficient technique possible for regaining what has been gathered over a long period of time, that is, discovery.

If we agree that at a particular point, evolution becomes Lamarckian in the sense of involving the passing on of acquired characteristics, not through the genes but through the medium of culture, this suggests to me that we had better be cautious in talking about the method of discovery, or discovery as the principal vehicle of education. Simply from a biological point of view, it does not seem to be the case at all. We ought to be extremely careful, therefore, to think about the range of possible techniques used for guaranteeing that we produce competent adults within a society that the educational process supports. Thus, in order to train these adults, education must program their development of skills, and provide them with models, if you will, of the environment. All of these things bring into serious question whether discovery is a principal way in which the individual finds out about his environment.

EXPLORING A SITUATION

You make no mistake if you take the phenomenon of language learning as a paradigm. Language learning is very close to invention and has very little in common with what we normally speak of as discovery. There are several things about language learning that strike me as being of particular interest. For example, in language learning, the child finds himself in a linguistic environment in which he comes forth with utterances. Take the first syntactic utterances. They usually have the form of a pivotal class and an open class, like "All gone, Mommy," "All gone, Daddy," and "All gone this; all gone that." The child, exposed linguistically to an adult world, comes forth not with a discovery but with an invention that makes you believe somewhat in innate ideas, in a linguistic form that simply is not present in the adult repertoire. Such language learning consists of invention or coming forth with grammar, possibly innately, that then becomes modified in contact with the world. The parent takes the child's utterances which do not conform to adult grammar. He then idealizes and expands them, not permitting the child to discover haphazardly but rather providing a model which is there all the time. It is the very earliest form of language learning.

Thus, within the culture the earliest form of learning essential to the person becoming human is not so much discovery as it is having a model. The constant provision of a model, the constant response to the individual's response after response, back and forth between two people, constitute "invention" learning guided by an accessible model.

If you want to talk about invention, perhaps the most primitive form of uniquely human learning is the invention of certain patterns that probably come out of deep-grooved characteristics of the human nervous system, with a lot of shaping taking place on the part of an adult. Consequently, wherever you look, you cannot really come away with a strong general consensus that discovery is a principal means of educating the young. Yet, the one thing that is apparent is that there seems to be a necessary component in human learning that is like discovery, namely, the opportunity to go about exploring a situation.

It seems to be imperative for the child to develop an approach to further learning that is more effective in nature—an approach to learning that allows the child not only to learn the material that is presented in a school setting, but to learn it in such a way that he can use the information in problem solving. To me, this is the critical thing: How do you teach something to a child? I am going to say teach even though I know that the word teaching is not very fashionable anymore. We talk about the child learning, or about programming the environment so that he can learn, but I want to raise the following question: How do you teach something to a child, arrange a child's environment, if you will, in such a way that he can learn something with some assurance that he will use the material that he has learned appropriately in a variety of situations?

TRANSFERABILITY AS LEARNING

The problem of how to teach a child in such a way that he will use the material appropriately again breaks down, for me, into six sub-problems.

First is the attitude problem. How do you arrange learning in such a way that the child recognizes that when he has information he can go beyond it, that there is connectedness between the facts he has learned with other data and situations? He must have the attitude that he can use his head effectively to solve a problem, that when he has a little bit of information he can extrapolate information; and that he can interpolate when he has unconnected material. Basically, this is an attitudinal problem—something that will counteract inertness in that he will recognize the material that he has learned as an occasion for moving beyond it.

Second is the compatibility problem. How do you get the child to approach new material that he is learning in such a fashion that he fits it into his own system of associations, subdivisions, categories, and frames of reference, in order that he can make it his own and thus be able to use the information in a fashion compatible with what he already knows?

Third involves getting the child activated so that he can experience his own capacity to solve problems and have enough success so that he can feel rewarded for the exercise of thinking.

Fourth is giving the child practice in the skills related to the use of information and problem solving. This is a highly technical problem that has to do not only with psychology but with learning those valuable short cuts within any field that we speak of as heuristics. I do not think that psychology stops at the level of psychological terminology, by any means, when we talk about learning in this particular context. But it is a feature of the thought process when a child learns some basic principles in mathematics he can use. Essentially, the tools of the mind are not only certain kinds of response patterns, but also organized, powerful tool concepts that come out of the field he is studying. There is no such thing, to be sure, as the psychology of arithmetic, but the great concepts of arithmetic are parts of the tool kit for thinking. They contain heuristics and skills that the child has to master. The great problem here is how do you give the child practice in the utilization of these skills—because it turns out that however often you may set forth general ideas, unless the student has an opportunity to use them he is not going to be very effective in their use.

Fifth is a special kind of problem that I want to speak of as "the self-loop problem." The child, in learning in school settings, will very frequently do kinds of things which he is not able to describe to himself. Psychologists see this all the time in new studies—children who are able to do many kinds of things, for example, to handle a balance beam quite adequately by putting rings on nails on both sides of a fulcrum and getting quite interesting balances, but are not able to say it to themselves and convert this fact into a compact notation which they could hold in mind.

The sixth problem involves the nature of our capacity for handling information flow manageably so that it can be used in problem solving.

Let me spell out these six problems in more detail, giving examples from *Man, A Course of Study*, earlier described in Chapter 3.

USING ONE'S OWN HEAD

First is the matter of attitude. Discovery teaching generally involves not so much the process of leading students to discover what is "out there," but rather, their discovering what is in their own heads. It involves encouraging them to say, Let me stop and think about that; Let me use my head; Let me have some vicarious trial-and-error. There is a vast amount more in most heads (children's heads included) than we are usually aware of, or that we are willing to try to use. You have got to convince students (or exemplify for them, which is a much better way of putting it) of the fact that there are implicit models in their heads which are useful.

Let me just say one thing about the attitude problem, to give you an example of how we try to have the children recognize that they can use their own heads in their own education. We wanted the children to learn that, generally speaking, one can reduce a language into what is called *type* and *order*. I, therefore, used a trick that I got from a suggestion of my colleague, George Miller, which consists of the following. First write a sentence on the board. Then get the children to form similar sentences as follows:

The	man	ate	his	lunch.
A	boy	stole	a	bike.
The	dog	chased	my	cat.
My	father	skidded	the	car.
A	wind	blew	his	hat.

At this particular point, we have the children provide other sentences *ad libitum*. And they provide them. Sometimes they are wrong. Usually not. We then shift them to the following puzzle: How is it that one can go from left to right across the sentences in practically any row and still come out with a sentence: *The boy chased the cat; A father chased a lunch; The man stole my bike; A father stole his hat.* Some of the sentences are rather silly, but clearly sentences. Soon they will say things like, There are five places and you can put lots of things in each place. But which kinds of words will fit into each column? Type and token begin to emerge as ideas. Now we reach a very critical point. Ask, for example, whether they can make up some more columns. One child proposed the following, something that put the class on a new level of attitude toward the use of mind. He said that there is a "zero" column that could contain the word "did." I asked what other particular words this column could contain. The children said, "did," "can," "has." This was the zero column. Then one of the pupils said that this did not quite fit and that you would have to change the word in the third column too but it would not be very much of a change. They were ready and willing now to get into the syntax of the language, to invent it afresh. They talked about the family of words that would fit and that two columns affected the families each could carry. Only then did we introduce some terminology. We talked about *type* and *order*, and that in sentences there were words that were types and they appeared in a certain permissible order. One of the children said of types, "They're called parts of speech. A noun, for example, is a 'person, place or thing.'" To produce a pause, we asked about "dying" and "courage." They were quick to grasp the syntactic distinction of "privilege of occurrence" in a certain position, in contrast to the semantic criterion of "person, place or thing" and found the idea interesting. They soon began on the alternative ways a sentence could be said and have the same meaning. We were soon building up the idea of productivity.

We were struck by the fact that once the children break into an idea in language, once they get a sense of a distinction, they quickly "turn around" on their own usage and make remarkable strides toward linguistic understanding. The only point I would make is that you must wait until *they* are willing reflectively to turn around before you begin operating with the abstractions. Otherwise they will become obedient and noncomprehending. In time, the habit of or attitude toward reflecting on what you habitually do or say becomes well established. I put this matter first for I feel that it is the one thing that children most rarely encounter in school—that it is a good practice to *use* their heads to solve a problem by reflecting on what they already know or have already learned. Are college students so different from fifth graders?

MAKING KNOWLEDGE ONE'S OWN

The compatibility problem is next in our list and it is interesting. I will describe it in terms of the behavior of some of our pupils. We were treating tool using as a problem. I would remind you that our children were suburban. They had not used many tools, nor thought much about what a tool is. A tool was something to get at the hardware store. Could we relate tools to something that they themselves knew about? Our aim was to present tools as amplifiers of human sensory, motor, and reflective powers—which includes mathematics in the range of tools.

To get the children away from their parochial notions about tools, we prepared a set of drawings of all kinds of tools and devised an exercise whose object was to restore some manner of awareness about tools. We would present a hammer. What is its use? One child said it is used for beating in nails. What do you want to drive in nails for? You drive nails in because you want to have the nail in the board. Why do you want to have the nail in the board? To hold two boards together. Why would you want two boards together? Well, to make a building steady or to support something like a table. Any other way to do it aside from hammer and nails? Yes, you could use string. String and nails do the same thing? And so on, and so forth. Along the way, it was quite apparent that when you got the pupils to rephrase uses in their own terms and kept pushing them as to how something could be used, eventually they would find some place where it connected with a structured body of knowledge they already had. This is what I mean by the "compatibility problem"—finding the connection with something they do know.

Frequently, we came upon some very striking surprises. Here are a couple of examples. One of the pictures was of a compass—the kind that is used for drawing circles. One child, a particularly interesting one, was asked about it. What is that for? It's a steadying tool. What do you mean, a steadying tool? She went to the board and took a piece of chalk. You see, if you try to draw a circle, you're not steady enough to make a real circle, so a compass steadies you. The other children thought the idea was great and came forth with a stream of suggestions for other steadying tools. One suggested a tripod for a camera. Another said a stick could be a steadying tool. He had seen a sign painter the other day, resting his arm on a stick.

I was struck by the fact that they were doing something very much like Wittgenstein's (1966) description of concept formation. Recall his description of a game. What is a game? There is no obvious hierarchical concept that joins tennis and tag. What these children were doing with steadying tools was forming a concept in which neighboring elements were joined by "family resemblance," to use Wittgenstein's phrase. The concept that emerges is like a rope in which no single fiber runs all the way through. The children are getting connections that allow them to travel from one part of the system to the other and when something new comes in, they find compatible connections. You can, at your peril, call it association. By calling it that you forget the systematic or syntactic nature of their behavior, as when they dealt with the idea of type and order in language. They were dealing with tools as governed by a rule of filling certain requirements—the different ways of getting steady or of holding things together. But the rules are not as simple as formal concepts. It is this kind of binding, this kind of exercise, that helps solve the compatibility problem, the problem of how to get a new piece of knowledge connected with an established domain so that the new knowledge can help retrieve what is likely to be appropriate to it as needed.

The compatibility problem turns out to have some surprising features. Let me illustrate by reference to a junior high school course: we deal with an episode in which Julius Caesar must decide whether to cross the Rubicon, leave Cisalpine Gaul to penetrate Italy, and try for Rome. The children have the commentaries of Caesar, nothing from Pompey who was Caesar's opponent, and letters from Cicero to various characters around Italy. The data are insufficient. The pupils must pull all the shreds together. Amusingly enough, the class divided into Caesarians and Pompeyans, comparing their heroes to people they knew about. The discussion was dramatic; they reasoned like politicians! Caesar *must* have had friends along there. He'd never have taken his army through a narrow valley like that if he hadn't some friends in there to count on! As a result, one group of pupils set off looking through Cicero's gossipy letters to find out whether Caesar might possibly have friends who had been passing information to him about the people along his narrow valley. The connections they were making were with their knowledge of the human condition and how people got on with each other. We did not care whether they made connections through the imagery of unsavory Boston politicians (with whom they at once equated Roman politicians). The interesting thing is that they connected. We tried out the

Caesar unit in a "problem" class in Melbourne, Florida—a group of leather-jacket motorcycle kids. They went completely for Caesar! They were exquisite analysts of the corrupt Roman system. Pompey just could not hold them. He was a fink without guts. The transcripts of these lessons are marvelous! It was only when they found the connection between Caesar and their strong-arm fantasies (and not always fantasies) that Rome and Melbourne came together. Forgive me for going on about something so obvious. It is just that it was not so obvious to us when we started.

COMPETENCE AS SELF-REWARDING

Consider activation now. I think that the reward that comes from using materials, discovering regularities, extrapolating, and so forth, is intrinsic to the activity. It probably goes beyond the satisfaction of curiosity. It has more to do with the form of motivation that Robert White (1959) speaks of as effectance or competence. Extrinsic rewards may mask this pleasure. When children expect a payoff from somebody, they tend to be drawn away from or distracted from the behavior that provides intrinsic rewards. You can corrupt them all too easily into seeking your favor, your rewards, your grades.

PROBLEM SOLVING THROUGH HYPOTHESIZING

Consider next the skill problem. It has had fewer surprises to it, but let me say a few things about it anyway. One of the skills is pushing an idea to its limit. For example, a question came up in one of our classes of how to get information from one generation to another. One fifth grader said that you did it by "tradition" and this empty formula satisfied most of the pupils. They were ready to go on to the next thing. I said that I did not quite understand what they meant by tradition. One child said that a tradition is that dogs chase cats. The others laughed. Well, the laughed-at boy responded, some people say it is an instinct, but he had a dog who did not chase cats until

he saw another dog do it. There was a long silence. The
children picked the issue up from there, reinvented the idea
of culture, destroyed the idea of instinct (even what is good
about it), ended up with most of their presuppositions rakishly
out in the open. Had I stopped the discussion earlier, we would
have been contributing to the creation of passive minds. What
the children needed were opportunities to test the limits of
their concepts. It often requires a hurly-burly that fits poorly
the decorum of a schoolroom. It is for this reason that I single
it out.

Training in the skill of hypothesis making has a comparable
problem. Here is an example of what I mean. We got into a
discussion in one of our classes of what language might have
been for the first speaking humans. We had already had a
similar session with one other class so I knew what was likely
to happen. Sure enough, one child said that we should go out
and find some "ape men" who were first learning how to speak
and then you would know. It is direct confrontation of a problem, and children age ten like this directness I was teaching
the class. I told the children that there were various people in
the nineteenth century who had traveled all over Africa on just
such a quest, and to no avail. Wherever people spoke, the
language seemed about the same in sophistication. They were
crestfallen. How could one find out if such ape men existed
any longer? I thought I should take drastic measures and present
them with two alternative hypotheses, both indirect. It is usually a fine way of losing a ten-year-old audience! They had the
week before been working on Von Frisch's bee-dance "language" so they knew a little about other than human forms of
communication. I proposed, as a first hypothesis, that to study
the origin of *human* language they look at some animal language
like bees and then at present human language, and perhaps *original* human language would be somewhere in between. That
was one hypothesis. I saw some frowns. They were not happy
about the idea. The other way, I proposed, was to take what was
simplest and most common about human language and guess
that those things made up the language man first started
speaking.

This discussion, weighing the worth of the two hypotheses,

took the whole period. What struck me was that in the course of the discussion the children were learning more how to *frame* hypotheses than how to test them, which is a great step forward. One child asked whether what would be simple in one language would necessarily be simple about another. They were trying to invent a hypothesis about language universals. Or another pupil suggested that the way babies speak is probably the way in which man first spoke. They enjoyed discussing not only whether the hypotheses were "true" but also whether they were testable. I told them finally that the Cercle Linguistique de Paris at the turn of this century had voted that nobody should be permitted to give a paper on the origin of human language, and that they were not doing badly, all things considered. They took a dim view of Paris as a result! I was struck by the avidity of the children for the opportunity to *make* hypotheses. I believe children need more such practice and rarely get it.

Training in being concise is, like limits testing and hypotheses making, a neglected though crucial area of skill training. I heard one fifth grader answer another who asked about a movie by starting off to recount it from the beginning. He was prepared to give a blow-by-blow account. They have little training in condensing information. I feel reasonably convinced that we could take a lesson from a game that Ford Maddox Ford and Joseph Conrad are alleged to have played on Sunday outings. Who could describe a landscape before them in the smallest number of words? I do not have much experience with this kind of training. All I do have is a sense of the overwhelming prolixity that gets in the way of the children I have observed.

THE SELF-LOOP PROBLEM

Consider now the fifth or "self-loop" problem. Edward Sapir once made the remark that language is a dynamo that we use principally for lighting little name plates, for labeling and categorizing things. When human beings some day learn how to use language effectively, we will probably spend much more

time probing the logical implications of how we say things. I
start the discussion of the self-loop with that thought.

Some examples: One child said to the class that all they were
doing that day was saying the same thing over and over in
different ways. Another child responded that the things in
question being talked about did not *say* the same thing. Still
another argued that they *were* the same thing. Now, the distinction between the syntactic and the semantic mode is not
easy at age ten. The children sensed, though, that the word
"same" needed to be decomposed into different kinds of sameness—a sameness of words and of things. It is not quite alike
to say of two intersubstitutable sentences that they are the
"same" form of sentence as to say that they are about the
"same" things.

Another instance happened quite by accident. A child,
smitten by the intersubstitutable sentences, put down a list
of two-word expletives:

jeepers	creepers
leaping	lizards
aw	gee
good	grief
my	goodness

I asked how they were alike. The children suggested you could
substitute in each column as with the sentences: "gee creepers,"
and "aw lizards," etc. It is an interesting kind of substitutivity.
But the more interesting thing is that some children said that
these phrases are the same though they do not stand for a
thing that is the same. If you speak of this as discovery, I
would agree. We would have to admit, however, that it is
not at all clear what was discovered. But the exercise is surely
a rich one!

THE POWER OF CONTRAST

The last point: How one engineers discovery, makes it more
workaday and less inspirational. One of the most powerful
tools we have for searching is contrast. Contrast can be

engineered or self-engineered. Indeed, it can become an acquired taste. We have gone out of our way to present material to children in contrastive form—film of baboon juveniles playing, followed by human children playing in an identical "habitat." The children discover quite readily that little baboons play mostly with little baboons and do not play with things, that human children play with things and with each other. This is engineering a situation. It provides a start for a discussion of tool use, free hands, and so on. Later, give them kittens (who play with things) and then have them deal anew with the problem. They will very quickly understand that cats play with things, but not by holding them.

We believe that by getting the child to explore contrasts, he is more likely to organize his knowledge in a fashion that helps discovery in particular situations where discovery is needed. I need not go into an elaborate justification of the method of contrast here, and will only note that its efficacy stems from the fact that a concept requires for its definition a choice of a negative case. Man is a different concept contrasted to standing bears, to angels, to devils. Readiness to explore contrasts provides a choice among the alternatives that might be relevant.

5

Toward a
Disciplined Intuition

In virtually any field of intellectual endeavor one may distinguish two approaches usually asserted to be different. One is intuitive, the other analytic. There are many ways in which the difference can be characterized, depending upon the particular field; but in general, intuition is less rigorous with respect to proof, more visual or ikonic, more oriented to the whole problem than to particular parts, less verbalized with respect to justification, and based upon a confidence in one's ability to operate with insufficient data. We will not attempt a more discerning definition of intuition at the juncture, but will assume, for the moment, that distinction is useful in characterizing approaches to intellectual work.

The solutions and discoveries of scientists and scholars are often at least partly intuitive. Science and history as written are the Sunday activities of the scientist and the historian in contrast to their weekday activities. It is also true that the leaps that man takes on the basis of insufficient evidence constitute the principal source of error in his intellectual activity. It is for this reason that thinking men, before stating their conclusion badly, shift to analysis to determine whether they were right or wrong in their short-cut approximations. Precise and demanding analysis is the guarantor against error.

Young children can be said to know things without being able to put what they know into words. This is where we find them when they enter school. If we take it as axiomatic or obvious that in teaching children we take them where we find them, it is quite plain that learning and teaching must start from some intuitive level. This may be true not only of young children entering the educational establishment for the first time, but of anybody approaching a new body of knowledge or skills for the first time. Only a romantic pedagogue would say that the main object of schooling is to preserve the child's intuitive gift. And only a foolish one would say that the principal object is to get him beyond all access to intuition, to make a precise analytic machine of him. Obviously, the aim of a balanced schooling is to enable the child to proceed intuitively when necessary and to analyze when appropriate.

It is with these considerations in mind that we turn to the question of how one brings a child to his full analytic powers in particular disciplines while at the same time preserving in him a robust sense of the uses of intuitive thinking, both in intellectual activities and in daily life.

FEATURES OF INTUITIVE THINKING

Better to assess the nature of the training that might nurture intuitive thinking, we turn here to a brief summary of some of its features that seem of particular importance in various intellectual disciplines: these are activation, confidence, visualization, nonverbal ability, the informal structuring of a task, and the partial use of available information.

1. Though it seems banal to say it outright, the first requirement of any problem-solving sequence is to get started, to
get behavior out where it can be corrected, to get the
learner committed to some track, to allow him to make an
external summary of his internal thought processes. One of
the first resistances to be overcome in problem solving is
inertia—"just sitting there," neither thinking much nor
doing anything. This is not to say that reflectiveness is not
a virtue at some point in the problem-solving sequence,
but reflectiveness serves better once there is some commitment to direction. Often a first precise move is not apparent
in solving a problem or in getting an idea straight. Rather,
one has the sense of a possible or estimated way of getting
started. It is almost a kind of locational activity, determining
what part of the forest to work in. It is in essence an im-
precise opening move that is involved.

2. While one must have some degree of self-confidence before
one can make a start on a task, the act of starting itself increases one's confidence in the ability to carry the task
through. Gifted teachers report often that their first task
is to give students the notion that their minds can be used
as instruments. The initial confidence of having made a
start and a sense of the problem's corrigibility (which we
shall discuss below) permits the learner, we would guess,
to move on to the task of formulating hypotheses on the
basis of partial evidence.

3. The paradigm or limit of most intuitive heuristics is direct
perception. When a person says that at last he "sees" something, often he means that he senses it in a visualized or
sensory embodiment. It is this kind of embodiment that
often permits directness of grasp or immediateness of conclusion. But it should also be clear that a visualization may
often be inappropriate. In any case, save in the rare instances of intuitive geometry, it is impossible to have a
rigorous proof of anything when it is in an ikonic form.
Yet, plainly, the visualization indicates in many cases what
one must do next to get it proved. "Seeing" something, un-
fortunately, carries with it the often false assumption that
something is as plain as seeing a thing out there. This is,
of course, a danger of unbridled intuition.

4. It is characteristic of intuitive procedures that the person
is not able to give much verbal justification of why he is

proceeding as he is or why he has made a particular discrimination. In this respect, the behavior is not fully under the control of the learner in the sense of being translatable into the language necessary for summary, transformation, and criticism. Justification in words or symbols or in manipulative proof is at least amenable to correction and closer analysis. But generally, the pure intuitive act is not so subject.

5. It is often assumed that intuitive thinking is somehow free and ungoverned. Surely this is a mistake. More likely, what we speak of as intuition is a shortcut based on an informal and often inexpressible structuring of a task. The structure, so-called, may be nothing more than a sense of a connection between means and ends or of some notion, difficult to clarify, of "belongingness."

6. Whether the person uses a heuristic involving visualization or some other shorthand way of summarizing the connections inside a set of givens, he drastically reduces the range of things to which he attends. This narrowing of focus involves a kind of risk taking that requires not only a certain amount of confidence, but also a kind of implicit rule for ignoring certain information, again a risky prescience about the nature of a solution or the kind of goal one is looking for. This is what imparts directionality to the subject's problem solving under these circumstances. The risk, of course, is in getting in so deep that it becomes hard to disengage and cut one's losses.

The foregoing are some of the aspects of intuition. This is not to suggest that they occur only as aspects of intuition, but that is a matter for closer analysis at some later time. Here a rough approximation suffices to get on with the task. Analysis should provide the correction, and to that subject we turn next.

ANALYSIS AND INTUITION

One can begin by noting that in a certain sense the opposite of the above characteristics holds—but only within limits. Analysis in a well-trained problem solver can be just as activating as intuition, but in many cases it takes a hunch to figure out first where the analytic tools should be applied. Similarly, analysis and a sense of one's capacity to apply analytic procedures increase a problem solver's confidence. Yet, at the same time, it is often a first order approximation, a nonrigorous proof showing that one is in the right domain, that gives one the confidence to go on with exacting and sometimes tedious analytic procedures of proof. Analytic, step-by-step proof requires a far more formulated structural sense of a problem, though the well-trained analyst may not be conscious of his structural assumptions while he is carrying out his task of verification.

The virtues of intuition as an opening approach to a problem are probably self-evident. One's first intuition, when faced with a new body of material, is often nothing more than a sense of "wrongness" or "rightness." I look at a list of projects planned for first graders learning about the Eskimo, for instance, and it strikes me at once that there is something wrong with some of the projects and something right about others. Putting plants in the icebox is right, but building a styrofoam igloo is wrong. By letting each item "speak" to me in a general way, I can categorize each project as right or wrong. But if I stop here, I am nowhere. Now it is time for analysis; I compare the lists, and, finally, the sense of wrongness is printed out as, say, "heavy-handed verisimilitude." Intuition, to be fruitful, must carry this sense of incompleteness, the feeling that there is something more to be done. It is most successful when it can be backstopped and disciplined by more rigorous techniques of problem-solving and problem formulation. For unless it operates in phase with more rigorous and verifiable methods, its deficiency is some combination of looseness and incorrigibility. Take for example the good intuitive formulation that, in order for international trade to exist, there must be some kind of exchange of goods and services between nations. It poses a problem in an interesting way. But if one stops with such a loose formulation, one is likely to miss out on the important boundary conditions that constrain this formulation. It fails to distinguish, for example, between a system marked by direct barter and one that involves a "delay" mechanism for balance of payments such as an international bank. Moreover, it fails to specify the manner in which a network of exchange can constitute an "internal market" of nations such as the British Commonwealth or the Common Market. The intuition, to be fully effective, must carry with it a way of analyzing exchange that goes beyond the first sense of economic mutuality. Many students who encounter such ideas as tariffs, economic relations, and the rest have only the analytic apparatus and none of the general intuitive feel that is needed to put the pieces into a coherent and understandable picture. Contrariwise, the student who rests solely with the idea of mutuality of trade has only the general image and none of the sense of how the mutuality works itself out in the complexities of the real world. The issue here is between understanding in an approximate way—having a sense of something—and being so lost in the particularities that the overall meaning of the relations among a set of facts is lost.

The issue is more complex than appears on the surface. For it does not hold that intuition is always vague and analysis always rigorous. It was not until quite recent years, for example, that Euler's famous "proofs" were rendered into rigorous form. In their original version many steps were left quite intuitive and, in a rigorous sense, untested and untestable. Yet much of mathematics was built upon them, and it took a century of living with the intuitive proofs for sufficient axiomatic skills to be developed to carry them to a point of rigor. One can extend this to mathematical understanding in the child. A young student may come to a clear understanding of factoring and prime numbers by visualizing them in terms of the way in which quantities of beans can or cannot be laid out in columns and rows. His understanding is clear but it is limited; it is difficult for him to relate it to other mathematical properties that cannot find an embodiment in the imagery that he has chosen to represent his ideas. Moreover, it is hard in any instance for the child, dealing with a moderately large number, to prove by bean arrangement alone that the number is or is not factorable.

But now take the case of intuition in a sphere where verifiability is not so accessible and where, possibly, it is of a different order. We could dip deep into the folk culture, for example, and take two popular comic strips—*Pogo* and *Little Orphan Annie*. Either can be read in terms of "what-happened-that-day." And probably a fair number of children read the strips in just that way. But one can also read each with a sense of its form of social criticism, its way of depicting human response to difficulty, its underlying assumptions about the dynamics of human character. One child is able to sense the underlying paternalistic authoritarianism of Little Orphan Annie or the gentle irony of Pogo with respect to authority. Another can give an accurate account of what went on over a period of a week in each strip. Surely we cannot call the second child more precise than the first; there is something he is not understanding at all. It is like those people who recount conversations in the "he said, she said" mode with no grasp of what in fact at some deeper level people were saying to each other. What one would hope to do for the child who had grasped the intuitive distinction between the two cartoon strips is to take him on to a richer understanding of what he had understood in this restricted domain. If his reading powers were up to it, we might lead him now to a reading of Jonathan Swift on the one hand and *Richard III* on the other. (Again, one could not hope at the outset for a deep mining of the vein of irony in *Gulliver*, nor for much of a grasp of Richard's contempt for man on the other.) Or possibly, in contrast to Daddy Warbucks, one would want to give the image of a type who, by his largesse, ends in a shambles of isolation—perhaps *Gatsby*. Whatever one chooses as the next episode in deepening a flickering intuition, it is certainly in the direction of extending it and refining it by exposure to new material.

Unexploited intuition that goes nowhere and does not deepen itself by further digging into the materials—be they human, literary, scientific, mathematical, political—is somehow not sufficient to bring the person to the full use of his capacities. Intuition is an invitation to go further—whether intuitively or analytically. And it is with the training of people to go further in this way that we are concerned here.

TRAINING OF INTUITION

Let it be said at the outset that nothing is known about the training of intuition and that very likely we are still too unclear about what is intended by the word to devise proper educational procedures. Yet paradoxically enough, there are features of the intuitive method that are fully enough appreciated and recognized—in an intuitive way, to be sure—to merit some consideration from the point of view not only of their educability but also from the point of view of how they may be linked with the kinds of "follow-up" acts that permit the exploitation of intuition.

Often, one of the first impressions that a child gets in school is that one proceeds by quite different techniques than one had hitherto used. There is a kind of damping down of fantasy, imagination, clever guessing, visualization, in the interest of teaching reading and drawing, writing and arithmetic. Great emphasis is placed upon being able to say what one has on one's mind clearly and precisely the first time. The atmosphere emphasizes "intraverbal skills"—using words to talk about words that refer to still other words.

Much has been said—much of it nonsense—on the need for building upon what the child already knows when designing a school curriculum. Start with the familiar friendly trashman, for example, before moving on to the rather more bizarre "community helpers" among the Netsilik Eskimo. However one feels about this question—and it seems doubtful to us that children really find pediatricians more interesting or even more comprehensible than witch-doctors—we are suggesting that transfer of skills the child has learned may be much more crucial to education than transfer of content. There is enough research now extant on children of the school-entering age to indicate that one can indeed build upon the skills that they bring to school with them, skills which, by our earlier definition, are clearly intuitive in nature. Consider a few of them.

We have commented earlier that intuitive operations precede highly descriptive or symbolic ones, and that one of the major forms of intuitive operation is somehow visual in nature. How can instruction help the child to exploit his visualizing skills and, more important, to begin to shape them into more rigorous instruments?

The young child makes no clear distinction between an object seen, the function to which it can be put, and the affect it arouses. Perhaps for this reason he has strong opinions as to which of two lines is angrier, wearier, or more exuberant. This sort of affective summarizing can be the basis for later discriminations between elegance and clumsiness in visual representations. Surely he should be allowed to practice these skills out in the open where they can be subjected to criticism.

There are numerous testing procedures which require the subject to decompose figures into their component parts—the Witkin test, for instance, and the Goldstein-Scheerer procedure. Such exercises are rarely used as instructional devices except in banal form as part of the "reading readiness" curriculum. A Danish investigator, Martin Johansen (1957), has shown that they can be used in a more sophisticated fashion: he is able to improve his subjects' understanding of solid geometry by giving them practice in decomposing complex solid forms into their component simpler solids. And various illustrators, notably the Dutch engraver Escher, have provided beautiful exercises in ambiguous decomposition of complex pictures.

There are a number of techniques which are used to test a child's recognition of transformations in images. The FLAGS procedure, for example, asks the child to choose, from a variety of complex flags in a variety of orientations, that one which matches the original. We would do well to train the child to recognize transformations rather than simply to test whatever facility he may have haphazardly acquired. We suspect that recognition of transformations is trainable: consider, for example, the fact that our children, growing up in a world thick with geometrical and mechanical constraints, early and permanently outstrip bush children in their ability to deal with visual mechanical problems.

Maria Montessori (1964) long ago described procedures for teaching children to make subtle sensory discriminations. Much could be done by way of training children to order differences which they discriminate, not simply in linear arrays but in multidimensional arrays. There is little question that techniques such as the game of tic-tac-toe played on Cartesian co-ordinates and multiple-classification games of a highly concrete nature do in fact enrich visual subtlety.

The child's graphic representational skills are highly diagrammatic in nature. They will soon become quite stereotyped and eventually take on conventional forms of representing "reality." In the first few years of schooling, it would be worthwhile to try to develop to some richer level the kinds of subjective diagrammatization that he already has within his grasp. There are conventional art forms that he, perhaps better than adults, is capable of penetrating—where size connotes centrality, for example: he produces pictures in which the teacher is enormous in terms of the space she occupies on the page, and little sister is scarcely more than a dot. Letting the child sense at the outset that this too is a permissible mode of representation and not simply a "cutely childish" form of drawing may provide him not so much with a new skill but with a sense that his old ways of knowing are neither indecent nor irrelevant. From here one can surely take the child to forms of graphic representation that discipline and use the forms of representation he has to communicate to other children.

The child who prays on the way to school, "Please, God, don't let them do Jules Verne in English class," seeks protection not from the subject matter of schooling but from its methods. He does not want a book that he has grasped intuitively and lovingly to come under the near sadistic dissections of his English teacher. So often the intuitive approach goes underground to become part of what David Page once called the "secret intellectual life" of the child. The result, one suspects, may not be the analytic facility aimed at by the educator but a loathing for seemingly arbitrary analysis and an uninformed intuition. The problem is most severe perhaps in the early school years, if only because prevention is so much easier than cure. But it is likely a persistent problem. One wonders, for example, whether the keen social intuitions of the junior high school student could not find their way into the social studies curriculum or into his reading of literature in school.

Allowing the child to use his intuitive faculties is not only a practical matter of exploiting available resources. It is also a matter of honesty. The overanalytic models so often presented to children in their textbooks on math and physics can lead to a confusion of proof and process. The Sunday hindsight physics of the textbook is often a far cry from the messy weekday activity of the real-life physicist, and makes physics seem more remote than it need be; children need models of competence, perhaps, but surely not of omnipotence. By recognizing the legitimacy of intuition as an intellectual operation, schools could spare their students the painful relearning that is required of them later when, for example, they "really get into" physics and are required not to prove a given solution but to find a solution. Find if you can any similarity between geography as presented in the usual textbook and geography as practiced by geographers. The problems are presented as solved at the outset. The child is then asked to consider how the "authority" arrived at his solution. In a geography text we will find at the beginning of a chapter the statement, "The world can be divided into temperate, torrid, and frigid zones." Virtually the whole of the effort in the paragraphs that follow is given over to making it seem as if this distinction is obvious. Many children, we are convinced, are left with the image of an earth in which one can find border signs which read, something of the order, "You are now entering the temperate zone," put there by some benign authority in league with the textbook writer. The problem, how to characterize the surface of the earth in terms of regions, disappears and geography is converted into a combination of tongue-twisting names in a gazeteer and some rather puzzling maps in which "Greenland looks much bigger than it is." What is lost in this arbitrariness is a development of a sense of problem in the child.

CONSTRAINT AND INTUITION

We have seen a teacher introduce a fifth-grade class to the game of "hidden numbers." Before the pupils enter the classroom, the teacher writes a set of numbers on the board and covers them up. He gives the students a few clues about the set—for example, that it sums to less than 20. It is up to the class to ask further questions about the numbers in order to infer what they are. In fact the game was a primitive version of algebra carried out in an intuitive fashion. One could not help but be struck by the way in which the children came to recognize the constraints of the information they had already received in guiding their guesses as to the nature of the numbers.

The same procedure is readily transferred to other spheres of intellectual activity. There is an almost infinite variety of games that can be played with an episode or a period of history. Indeed, even so superficially unpromising a subject as geography can be converted into the form of making inference from partial information—a central feature of intuitive procedure. What is needed at this juncture is careful observational research on what children actually do in learning to play such "games" skillfully and in what ways they can be led to transfer their skills in a general way to other fields.

Most important of all is the basic question as to whether training of this kind might lead the child to greater confidence in intellectual activity generally. After all, the great question in training a mind to operate beyond the sphere of intellectual involvement of a formal kind is precisely to train it to reach conclusions on the basis of insufficient evidence and to know how to inquire after new evidence in order to cut down the conjectural nature of the conclusions he has reached.

GOING BEYOND THE INFORMATION GIVEN

Most human beings are unaware of how much information they actually possess on a given subject. Put more technically, when information is organized in terms of some generative model, it turns out that there are many other things that follow from it in a way that verges on redundancy. While this is usually recognized in more structured subjects such as mathematics (we all grant that the statement "Alice is taller than Mary; Mary is taller than Jane" implies that Alice is taller

than Jane), it is not so generally recognized that any connected
body of knowledge contains such redundant implications, even
if in a less strict sense. What does one know, for example,
about situations in which a group of people are being taxed
by officials over which they have no electoral control or no
other recourse? Surely, something more than that a popular
cry of the Revolution was "No taxation without representation."

Again we feel that there are many exercises that can have
the effect of leading the child to recognize not only that he
has a string of facts but that, put into some order, they generate
more facts. This is the notion behind much recent urging that
curricula be organized around the idea of the structure of
a discipline. But the matter goes well beyond that. Indeed,
well short of a "discipline," most collections of givens have
about them the character of a substructure which, when sensed,
provides the way of going beyond the information given.

It has often been said that structural considerations of this
sort are more relevant to sciences and mathematics than to
literature or history. It seems that this is likely a misunder-
standing of what is meant by structure. If a novel is put together with no necessary relation between one set of events and
others, then surely it is a poor novel. Consider, for example,
the crew of the Pequod in *Moby Dick*. Why are they all pagans,
not a Christian in the lot? What if they had all been New
Bedford Puritans—even libertine Puritans? It is this pagan
crew that searches the white whale to the deepest part of the
sea. Why is the whale white and the crew pagan? And what
manner of man would Ahab have to be? What other kind of
captain could have commanded such a quest? Melville wrote
to Hawthorne that this was a wicked book, suggesting indeed
that it was concerned with subversive matters. We are not
proposing that children be turned early toward the symbol-
chasing proclivities of the new criticism. Rather, the object
here is to suggest that in this work of art there is something
that lies beyond the mere narrative.

Consider the nature of a play. Can the third act drift off
independently of the first two? Likely not. A student who has
pondered the first two acts should be able to write a reasonably
appropriate third act—though it may differ from the original.

In comparing his version with the playwright's, the student should become aware of subtle constraints that he did and did not take into account. Here "error" can be extremely informative: Was the student carried away by the desire for a happy ending or for one that carried a bang when a whimper would have been more appropriate?

HEURISTIC ECONOMY

There are ways for using the mind in a fashion designed to save work, to make seemingly difficult problems easier, to bring a complicated matter into the range of one's attention. One rarely speaks of them, and surely there are no courses for teaching them. One learns to make little diagrams or to use a matrix. Or one asks oneself whether the solution he is tending toward will have a magnitude that is somewhere within the range of magnitudes in which the correct solution lies. Or one asks, encountering a new problem, whether there is anything like it one has encountered and solved before. Or one asks where one is trying to get. Or asks, how would I act if I were a molecule? Or, before doing the experiment we ask what would we know if it came out in one extreme way as compared to another. All of these are ways of honoring the fact that man has highly limited capacities for attending to things, for remembering them, or, in general, for processing information.

In general the difference between two people of equal IQ, one of whom is bright and the other stupid, is that the first has learned how to use his limited capacities by conserving them, by not straining after gnats, by cutting his losses early, by taking a little thought before committing himself to a long chain of reckoning. Most such economical heuristics are subject-specific—or seemingly so. But some experiments indicate that surprisingly large gains can be scored by teaching them even in a manner not related to specific subject matters, as in the experiments of Covington, Crutchfield, and Davies (1966). What is quite plain is that students can be trained out of their use by schoolmasters who regard such techniques as forms of cheating. They are the ones who value precision in procedure more highly than solution of a problem. Housewives are told to use the fruits of time and motion studies in refining their bed-making procedures. Why should efficient algebra be regarded as a sin?

We would suggest as a start that any new curriculum contain a syllabus designed to teach the economical tricks of the trade as early and as effectively as possible. We should also like to propose that special research be undertaken to devise and test certain "transcurricular" courses that have as their object the teaching of such methods. Efforts at inquiry training, at teaching students to attend to and use the cues that are available, and the like have proved sufficiently successful to warrant an effort of this sort. If nothing else were accomplished by such a program, at least it would signal that it is not disgraceful or lazy to save one's heels by using one's head.

Let one thing be clear in conclusion. The urgent proposal that the ways of teaching intuition be studied with great care comes out of a conviction that intuition is not only fruitful but necessary. The young child approaching a new subject or an unfamiliar problem either has recourse to the less than rigorous techniques of intuition or is left motionless and discouraged. So too the scientist or critic operating at the far reach of his capacities in his chosen field. The proposal does not assume that intuition and its uses should be encouraged in untrammeled form; rather it suggests that intuitive skill be used and exploited and that it be buttressed by more rigorous followups. If a man is to use his capacities to the full and with the confidence that fits his powers, he has no alternative but to recognize the importance and power of intuitive methods in all fields of inquiry—literature and mathematics, poetry and linguistics.

There is one final consideration. The development of computing devices will in years ahead serve to amplify enormously man's capacity for analysis; indeed, such devices are amplifiers for analytic thinking. This raises two related questions. The first has to do with the impact of technology on man's thinking. Cultural history indicates that man's ways of thinking are conditioned by the tools that he has at his disposal, for the tools become incorporated into his very thought process. They are the "print-out" to which he is geared. Yet paradoxically enough, it may well be that computers, in addition to expanding the power of analytic thinking, will also pose a need for greater and greater intuitive power. For the issue of how to use computing devices—their range and form of applicability—will itself pose a problem that can only be approached at first by intuitive means. In an age when man has developed machinery to run off the routine analytic tasks, it may well be that his best alternative is to develop inventive powers for dealing with the ill-formed and partly formed problems that remain. It is precisely in this domain that a vigorous and courageous intuitive gift, refined through practice, can serve man best.

6

Culture, Politics, and Pedagogy

Despite the books and articles that are beginning to appear on the subject, the process of education goes forward today without any clearly defined or widely accepted theory of instruction. We have had to make do and are still making do on clever maxims and moralistic resolutions about what instruction is and should be. The controversy that swirls around this tortured subject is a mirror of larger discontent with our culture and our morality. And so it should be—but not to the exclusion of dispassionate appraisal of the means whereby the sought-after ends might be achieved. And perhaps that, too, is overly much to expect, for if the past decade has taught us anything, it is that educational reform confined only to the schools and not to the society at large is doomed to eventual triviality.

There are a number of reasons why a theory of instruction may have little effect on educational practice. First, it could be that the theory is wrong—yet it is difficult to find a theory that is flat wrong and won't have some reasonable proposals to make. A second reason might be that it is inappropriate to the central problems of practice. For instance, a theory that is clearly excellent in respect to the instruction of children who are already motivated to learn may prove ineffective in dealing with the alienated Negro students of the inner-city school. A third reason might be its unmanageability—one aspect of which is obscurity in the path from the abstract to the concrete. No matter how deeply one is moved by the spirit of Froebel's theory (1890), for example, it is difficult to know what one does to assure, in his metaphor, that a child be nurtured like a plant lest he be choked by the weeds of circumstance.

But even if a pedagogical theory is correct, relevant, and manageable, it may be practically ineffective when it fails to relate to the urgencies of a society.

While American society in the first decades of the twentieth century was deeply concerned with the problem of acculturating new waves of immigrants, the favored theories were more concerned with the teaching of content per se, with minimum emphasis upon formal discipline or the training of mental faculties. Such theories were perhaps too closely related to the education of special elites. Today they are popular again. Our problem, however, is no longer that of creating a common background, but rather of controlling a complex social technology.

A theory fares well when it accords with a culture's conception of its function. Each culture has conceptions of the nature of a child, some conceptions of what constitutes good adults. It also has, at some implicit level, some conception of what it regards as the appropriate means of getting from the nature of a child to the nature of an adult. If a pedagogical theorist is to move that culture, he must forge a theory that relates to that range of acceptable means. The failure of a theory may be that it fails to accord with or overcome or relate to the "range of acceptable means" of a culture.

The net outcome of our probing is, I think, the realization that a pedagogical theory is perforce quite different from, and hardly as neutral as, the usual type of scientific theory. Indeed, it is even questionable whether it is principally a scientific theory in the explanatory sense. Nor is it a purely normative theory such as a grammatical theory, prescribing rules for reaching specified goals (such as "well formed sentences"). A theory of instruction is a political theory in the proper sense that it derives from consensus concerning the distribution of power within the society—who shall be educated and to fulfill what roles? In the very same sense, pedagogical theory must surely derive from a conception of economics, for where there is division of labor within the society and an exchange of goods and services for wealth and prestige, then *how* people are educated and in what number and with what constraints on the use of resources are all relevant issues. The psychologist or educator who formulates pedagogical theory without regard to the political, economic, and social setting of the educational process courts triviality and merits being ignored in the community and in the classroom.

It is neither surprising nor inappropriate, then, that critiques of pedagogical theories are as often as not in the form of social and political criticism and ideological debate. It has been instructive to me to see the manner in which some of these debates take shape. A book of mine, *The Process of Education* (1960), has been translated into several languages. In Italy, the book touched off a debate on the problem of revising Italian education to cope with the changing industrial society, and it has been used for clubbing Marxists and classicists alike. In the Soviet Union, one group of social critics has used the book's emphasis on discovery and intuition to castigate the dogmatism of remaining Stalinists who wish to set the dogma of socialism on the line in the classroom. That view has been seconded in Poland, Hungary, and Czechoslovakia.

In Japan, the social critics praise the book for indicating that school subjects that are technical and mathematical need not be without a proper intellectual structure and cultural grace. In Israel, a land surrounded by a ring of hostile nations, the book has been greeted as an invitation to avoid mediocrity in the preparation of new immigrants—a mediocrity that social critics fear will bring Israel to a state of dangerous vulnerability in her present isolated position. In the United States—and perhaps this is the only country affluent enough to harbor such thoughts—the principal social criticism has been a concern for the maintenance of spontaneity of the child. It has been a sobering experience to realize in what degree a book of this sort must perforce serve social and political ends and can never remain a technical book alone.

This brings me to a second conclusion, this time about the role of manageability in the impact of pedagogical theories. Manageability encompasses not only the so-called educational technology of films, books, computers, and the like, but also the scale of the enterprise in terms of people and funds. We have now entered an era in which the federal government, through the Office of Education, has established regional research and development centers to concern themselves with the betterment of our educational effort. They provide a fresh opportunity to explore deeply the feasibility of particular theories, comprehensive or segmental, concerning effective instruction.

I have had the intimate experience over the last five or six years of participating in and observing the attempt to translate a more general theory into one single course in the social sciences, "Man: A Course of Study" (1965), designed for the fifth grade. The experience has taught us all not to be casual about means. For it soon turns out that what seems like a simple pedagogical premise would, if implemented, produce a minor revolution in teacher training or in film making or in school budgeting. This is the engineering part of what is properly called the theory of instruction. It is something that we are only now beginning to understand. Innovation, by whatever theoretical derivation, involves vast development and engineering. By past standards of performance, we could not absorb many new innovative ideas. If we learn how to implement these matters in our generation, we shall lay the groundwork for a truly great impact of adequate theories of instruction in the next generation.

EDUCATION AS A WAY OF LIVING

These observations on why theories of instruction are ineffective lead to a second question: What is it that is special or different about education in the sense of schooling in contrast to other ways in which we instruct?

It takes learning out of the context of immediate action just by dint of putting it into a school. This very extirpation makes learning become an act in itself, freed from the immediate ends of action, preparing the learner for the chain of reckoning, remote from payoff that is needed for the formulation of complex ideas. At the same time, the school (if successful) frees the child from the pace-setting of the round of concrete daily activity. If the school succeeds in avoiding a pace-setting round of its own, it may be one of the great agents for promoting reflectiveness. Moreover, in school, one must "follow the lesson," which means one must learn to follow either the abstraction of written speech—abstract in the sense that it is divorced from the concrete situation to which the speech might originally have been related—or the abstraction of language delivered orally but out of the context of an ongoing action. Both of these are highly abstract uses of language. It is no wonder, then, that many recent studies report large differences between "primitive" children who are in schools and their brothers who are not: differences in perception, abstraction, time perspective, and so on.

As a society becomes yet more technical, there is a longer separation from actual doing, and education begins to take up a larger and larger portion of the life span; indeed, education becomes part of the way of life. More and more time is given over to telling (usually in print), to demonstrating out of the context of action.

We can already forsee a next step in technical progress that will impose further changes on our methods of educating. For one thing, the rate of change in the surface properties of knowledge will likely increase. That is, the theory of circuits will blossom, although likely as not it will do so on the basis of understanding more deeply some principles that are now known but not fully understood. In teaching, then, we shall be more likely to search out the deeper, underlying ideas to teach, rather than presenting the technical surface that is so likely to change. A metaphoric way of putting this is to say that technical things are more likely to appear changed to an engineer than to a physicist.

There will also be many more aids and prosthetic devices for processing information than ever before. Some of these seem certain already. For one thing, we are organizing our knowledge in a data bank accessible to a user by retrieval techniques inherent in modern computing. This makes knowledge more accessible and less subject to the ancient filing and recall gymnastics of the classical scholar. For another, there will be increasing pressure to reformulate problems in a well-formed fashion in order to make them accessible to the powerful devices of computing. Ill-formed problems do not lend themselves to computing. There are dangers and opportunities in such formalism. Whichever, the trend is already discernible. In general, I think it can be said that we shall in the next hundred years be using many more intelligent and automatic devices that we shall program in behalf of our problem solving. We need not be Luddites about it, either.

EDUCATING FOR THE FUTURE

I suspect that there are three forms of activity that no device is ever going to be able to do as well as our brain with its 5×10^9 cortical connections, and I would suggest that these three represent what will be special about education for the future.

The first is that we shall probably want to train individuals not for the performance of routine activities that can be done with great skill and precision by devices, but rather to train their individual talents for research and development, which is one of the kinds of activities for which you cannot easily program computers. Here I mean research and development in the sense of problem finding rather than problem solving.

If we want to look ahead to what is special about a school, we should ask how to train generations of children to *find* problems, to look for them. I recall that wonderful prescription of the English Platonist, Weldon, to the effect that there are three kinds of things in the world: There are troubles which we do not know quite how to handle; then there are puzzles with their clear conditions and unique solutions, marvelously elegant; and then there are problems—and these we invent by finding an appropriate puzzle form to impose upon a trouble.

What this entails for education is necessarily somewhat obscure although its outlines may be plain. For one thing, it places a certain emphasis on the teaching of interesting puzzle forms: ways of thinking that are particularly useful for converting troubles into problems. These are familiar enough in any given field of knowledge: they are the useful abstractions. What is needed is a sense of how to teach their use in converting chaotic messes into manageable problems. Much of the attraction of the use of discovery in teaching comes, I suspect, from the realization of the need to equip students in this way.

A second special requirement for education in the future is that it provides training in the performance of "unpredictable services." By unpredictable services, I mean performing acts that are contingent on a response made by somebody or something to your prior act. Again, this falls in the category of tasks that we shall do better than automata for many years to come. I include here the role of the teacher, the parent, the assistant, the stimulator, the rehabilitator, the physician in the great sense of that term, the friend, the range of things that increase the richness of individual response to other individuals. I propose this as a critical task, for as the society becomes more interdependent, more geared to technological requirements, it is crucial that it not become alienated internally, flat emotionally, and gray. Those who fret and argue that we are *bound* to go dead personally as we become proficient technically have no more basis for their assertion than traditional romanticism. Recall that the nineteenth century that witnessed the brunt of the Industrial Revolution also produced that most intimate form, the modern novel.

Third, what human beings can produce and no device can

is art—in every form: visual art, the art of cooking, the art of love, the art of walking, the art of address, going beyond adaptive necessity to find expression for human flair.

These three—research and development, unpredictable services, and the arts—represent what surely will be the challenge to a society which has our capacity to provide technical routine. I assume we shall teach the technical routines, for that is built into our evolving system. Will we be daring enough to go beyond to the cultivation of the uniquely human?

EDUCATION FROM THE OUTSIDE IN

Another question we must ask, then, is: How can the power and substance of a culture be translated into an instructional form?

First of all, it becomes necessary to translate bodies of theory into a form that permits the child to get closer and closer approximations to the most powerful form of a theory, beginning with a highly intuitive and active form of a theory and moving on as the child grasps that to a more precise and powerful statement of it. I find no other way of bringing the child through the maze of particulars to the kind of power that would produce the combination of research and development, unpredictable services, and the arts. Second, this means that on a practical level the entire university community—indeed, the entire intellectual community—must have a role in education, that the separate education faculty is a misconception and probably one that requires rearrangement in the future. (Since this was written, Cornell has disbanded its faculty of education and reassigned its responsibilities to the entire faculty of arts and sciences.)

Now if this is the case, there is surely need for a *special* coalition to devise means of teaching the symbolic activity involved in the kind of theory making we have been discussing. I do not know what to call this coalition of fields; the symbol sciences might be appropriate, but it is an absurd name. Linguists, philosophers of science, philosophers of history, logicians, psychologists, teachers, substantive specialists who most understand the simple structures of their fields, mathematicians—such a coalition might show how a university might express its concern for the symbolic powers inherent in the use of a culture. We obviously do not understand what could be done by a group of this sort. They range all the way from teaching children to be brief and compact when that is needed to hold things in the range of attention, to devising the kind of mathematical program embodied in the report of the Cambridge Conference on School Mathematics (1963).

But, you may ask, how do we get the teacher trained to "get across" these powerful ideas. The answer is surely *not* by conventional teacher training (cf. Silberman, 1970).

It is a simple suggestion I would make. Entering the culture is perhaps most readily done by entering a dialogue with a more experienced member of it. Perhaps one way in which we might reconsider the issue of teacher training is to give the teacher training in the skills of dialogue—how to discuss a subject with a beginner. There is a Russian proverb to the effect that one understands only after one has discussed. There are doubtless many ways in which a human being can serve as a vicar of the culture, helping a child to understand its points of view and the nature of its knowledge. But I dare say that few are so potentially powerful as participating in dialogue. Professor Jan Smedslund, at Oslo, has recently remarked on our failure to recognize that even in the domains of formal reasoning, logic, and mathematics, the social context of discussion can be shown to be crucial.

Pedagogical theory, then, is not only technical but cultural, ideological, and political. If it is to have its impact, it must be self-consciously all of these. The technical task, indeed, is more formidable than ever we suspected, and we may now be operating close to the scale where we can begin to do the appropriate engineering to realize the implications of even utopian theories.

Knowledge, to be useful, must be compact, accessible, and manipulable. Theory is the form that has these properties. It should be the aim of our teaching. But in the evolution of education, it is also the case that as we move to an ever more technical organization of our culture, and now to a period involving the use of information-processing automata, the pattern of education changes. Three uniquely human traits want especial cultivation to increase the human quality of human societies —problem finding, the provision of unpredictable services, and art in its myriad forms from music to cuisine.

Finally, one of the most crucial ways in which a culture provides aid in intellectual growth is through a dialogue between the more experienced and the less experienced, providing a means for the internalization of dialogue in thought. The courtesy of conversation may be the major ingredient in the courtesy of teaching.

7

The Relevance of
Skill or the Skill of
Relevance

About a decade ago I became actively involved in what was to
become known as the "curriculum-reform movement" in American education. The initial objectives were simple yet appealing
in their aspiration. The teaching of science (and that was the
founding concern soon to be generalized to other subjects)
must be made to represent what science was about so that
modern man might have some better sense of the forces that
shaped his world. The underlying conception was a rationalistic
one: By knowing nature and being adept in the ways of thinking of science and mathematics, man would not only appreciate
nature, but would feel less helpless before it, and would
achieve the intellectual dignity inherent in "being his own
scientist."

The moment that one says that physics should be taught not to spectators but to participants, that we should teach physics rather than teach *about* physics, then the physicist must be brought into the process as curriculum maker, along with the teacher. For the basic assumption is that physics is not so much the *topic* as it is the mode of thought, an apparatus for processing knowledge about nature rather than a collection of facts that can be got out of a handbook.

What is meant when we say that physics (or mathematics or a language or some other subject) is not something that one "knows about" but is, rather, something one "knows how to"? Plainly, one is neither quite committing something to memory to be tested by the usual means, nor is one learning to perform upon presentation of a cue like a trained seal or one of Professor Skinner's pigeons. Rather, when one learns physics, one is learning ways of dealing with givens, connecting things, processing unrelated things so as to give them a decent order. It is a way of connecting what one observes and encounters so as to highlight its redundancy, and therefore to make it as obvious as possible. To use what has now become a familiar phrase, it is an approach to learning that emphasizes ways of getting from the surface of the observed to its underlying structure of regularity. In this sense, it is a constant exercise in problem formulating and problem solving.

Good "problems," it turns out on closer inspection, are the chief vehicle for good curricula, whether one is in an ordinary classroom or alone in a cubicle with a teaching machine. In the main, formulated problems are of two kinds. One has to do more with the formal or analytic structure of the operation— the syntax of the subject. Being able to express acceleration for a set of velocities in an equation, or showing wherein Snell's law for the pressure of light must or must not be a necessary corollary of the conservation theorems—these are examples of exercises principally with the syntactic structure of a body of knowledge. They are problems that relate to logical implications, identity, equivalence, and transformational rules. They are mustered by considering the language and the notational system, and not by looking at rocks and trees. They have a counterpart in the social sciences. Did slavery "cause" the Civil War or were the two of them reflections of some deeper trend? What is implied by the term "military-industrial complex"? In what sense are tennis, blackjack, and love all "games"? Is it proper to define a weekend as any sequence of days including one and only one Sunday?

There is a second set of problems that has to do principally with the semantic aspect of a science. How high is some particular building, or what temperature is needed to desalinate a certain volume of seawater, or what is the perturbation around a foil passing through a given medium, given such and such Reynolds number? Or how are suicides and the Gross National Product correlated? There is involved here some form of determination of a value, a way of getting access cannily to a physical or social phenomenon. Looking at rocks and trees and incomes and populations is very much at the heart of it, but looking at them with a highly assisted eye turns out to be central. A good field is one where one doesn't have to go about making such empirical determinations very often, and we know that things are getting better when we can reconstruct how something should be from what is already known rather than being a brave and naked empiricist.

We come to treasure problems of both types: the former are "think" problems, the latter are laboratory or observational exercises. Both are formulated by the instructor, the text, or the manual, and both are important in any science, art, or practical sphere.

But neither is much like problem finding. When Hahn and Strassman made their fundamental discovery about the transmutation of uranium under certain conditions of bombardment, they wrote that they were unsure how to cope with the surprise of an element changing its atomic weight, which is possible only in alchemy. It was the implausibility rather than the improbability that shook them—as with bridge hands, all of which are equally improbable, but one in a single suit is implausible while a Yarborough of the same probability escapes attention altogether as extraordinary. One has no doubt whatsoever that the hare can overtake the tortoise. Problem finding comes when one senses that there remain some dark problems about whether a divisibility rule may not be consistent with another rule about minimal invariant units in ordinary algebra. Nor is it plain that the invention of the calculus resolves Zeno's paradox once for all. All of these are matters involving the raising of problems, rather than their solution. They require many of the same skills and the same knowledge of underlying regularity of problem solving. But they basically require the location of incompleteness, anomaly, trouble, inequity, and contradiction.

In none of what we have described thus far is there anything like memorization or performing a particular repertory. Conventional learning theories have little to do with the matter and it seems inconceivable that there stands between you and understanding a missing word of praise or a chocolate bar. Rather, what seems to be at work in a good problem-solving "performance" is some underlying competence in using the operations of physics or whatever, and the performance that emerges from this competence may never be the same on any two occasions. What is learned is competence, not particular performances. Any particular performance, moreover, may become "stuck" or overdetermined by virtue of having been reinforced. It is like the wicked schoolboy trick of smiling when the teacher utters a particular word, and before long the teacher is using it more often. But to confuse that phenomenon with language is as much of a mistake as confusing the trained seal piping "Yankee Doodle" with the improvisation of a variation on the piano.

You may by now have recognized the parallel between what I am suggesting and what we have come to know about language comprehension and production, and their acquisition. Learning to be skillful with a body of knowledge is much like learning a language, its rules for forming and transforming sentences, its vocabulary, its semantic markers, etc. As with language, there is also the interesting feature in all such learning that what is learned is initially "outside" the learner—as a discipline of learning, as a subject matter, as a notational system. This we shall examine later.

It has been the long-established fashion among traditionally anti-mentalist psychologists to dodge the issue of skill and competence by asserting that, while common sense may see it this way, the "real" explanation of learning is to be found at the molecular level of discrete stimuli and responses and their connections and reinforcements and generalization. What goes on at the commonsense level, as ordinary learning would be called, is simply a matter of engineering, a case of figuring out how to put the elements together in the right way by the correct contingencies of reinforcement or the management of contiguities. I believe this to be a wildly mistaken model of learning based on some very erroneous ideas that have stood up very poorly to the test of the laboratory or of the classroom.

What is meant when we say that human beings learn skills? The simplest form of skill is sensorimotor (tool using, car driving, etc.), and its form of acquisition has been described with increasing precision over the past quarter-century by Sir Frederic Bartlett and his students—Craik, Broadbent, Welford, and others. In broad outline, skilled action requires recognizing the features of a task, its goal, and means appropriate to its attainment; a means of converting this information into appropriate action, and a means of getting feedback that compares the objective sought with present state attained. This model is very much akin to the way in which computerized problem solving is done, and to the way in which voluntary activity is controlled in the nervous system. The view derives from the premise that responses are not "acquired" but are constructed or generated in consonance with an intention or objective and a set of specifications about ways of progressing toward such an objective in such a situation. In this sense, when we learn something like a skill, it is in the very nature of the case that we master a wide variety of possible ways for attaining an objective—many ways to skin the cat. For we learn ways of constructing many responses that fit our grasp of what is appropriate to an objective.

One is able to operate not only upon the world of physical objects by the use of sensorimotor skills, but also to operate in a parallel fashion upon that world as it is encoded in language and other more specialized symbol systems. For such symbol systems "represent" the world and the relations that hold between its different aspects. Indeed, this is what is so extraordinary about the power to symbolize—precisely that it has this representative function (a matter that surely vexes philosophers, in spite of the boon it bestows on ordinary men). This is what makes the "external" forms of systems like natural language or mathematics or a scientific discipline such powerful tools of culture. By making them part of our own symbolic skill, we are able to use them internally as instruments of our own thought. Physics become now an operation of the human mind, and physics thinking becomes a psychological topic. It is an instrument of thought or a skill rather than a "topic."

It was basically this set of convictions that led those of us who were in the midst of curriculum reform to propose that *doing* physics is what physics instruction should be about—even if the instruction had very limited coverage. And we proposed that doing it from the start was necessary, even if at the outset the student had only the vaguest intuition to fall back upon. The basic objective was to make the subject your own, to make it part of your own thinking—whether physics, history, ways of looking at painting, or whatnot. There follows from this view of competence as the objective of education some rather firm conclusions about educational practice. To begin with, a proper curriculum in any subject (or in the total curriculum of the school) requires some statement of objectives, some statement of what kinds of skill we are trying to create and by what kinds of performances we shall know it. The essence of such behavioral objectives is the specification of a test of skill—testing the ability to get to an objective in situations and with materials not yet encountered.

Does it sound familiar? Is it not what was initially intended? How did we get so far off the track in setting up our educational practices? Why was this rather simple notion not followed up? I suspect that part of the difficulty was introduced by wrongly focused theories of learning that lost sight of the forest of skilled competence for the trees of perfected performances. But that is only part of it. There is a very crucial matter about acquiring a skill—be it chess, political savvy, biology, or skiing. The goal must be plain; one must have a sense of where one is trying to get to in any given instance of activity. For the exercise of skill is governed by an intention and feedback on the relation between what one has intended and what one has achieved thus far—"knowledge of results." Without it, the generativeness of skilled operations is lost. What this means in the formal educational setting is far more emphasis on making clear the purpose of every exercise, every lesson plan, every unit, every term, every education. If this is to be achieved, then plainly there will have to be much more participatory democracy in the formulation of lessons, curricula, courses of study, and the rest. For surely the participation of the learner in setting goals is one of the few ways of making clear where the learner is trying to get.

This brings us directly to the problem of relevance, that thumb-worn symbol in the modern debate about the relation of education to man and society. The word has two senses. The first is that what is taught should have some bearing on the grievous problems facing the world, the solutions of which may affect our survival as a species. This is social relevance. Then there is personal relevance. What is taught should be self-rewarding by some existential criterion of being "real," or "exciting," or "meaningful." The two kinds of relevance are not necessarily the same, alas.

I attended a meeting in Stockholm in the summer of 1969, convened by the Nobel Foundation with the object of bringing scholars and scientists together to discuss the burning issues of the day. We had in attendance as well a panel of university students to voice their own concerns. I recall one session at which two molecular biologists, Joshua Lederberg of Stanford and Jacques Monod of Paris, were discussing the socially risky and morally compelling problems involved in improving man's genetic makeup with the aid of modern molecular biology. When the discussion was nearing its end, several students expressed disappointment in our avoidance of "relevant issues." Why had we not engaged ourselves with the crucial issues of the day: with the developing world, with the population explosion, with the scourge of war?

Jacques Monod replied with Gide's favorite proverb: "Good intentions make bad literature." I would change it to "Good intentions alone . . ." For it is precisely, again, a question of skill and understanding that is at issue. I am with those who criticize the university for having too often ignored the great issues of life in our time. But I do not believe that the cure in the classroom is to be endlessly concerned with the immediacy of such issues—sacrificing social relevance to personal excitement. Relevance, in either of its senses, depends upon what you know that permits you to move toward goals you care about. It is this kind of "means-ends" knowledge that brings into a single focus the two kinds of relevance, personal and social. It is then that we bring knowledge and conviction together, and it is this requirement that faces us in the revolution in education through which we are going.

I have suggested that the human, species-typical way in which we increase our powers comes through converting external bodies of knowledge embodied in the culture into generative rules for thinking about the world and about ourselves. It is by this means that we are finally able to have convictions that have some consequences for the broader good. Yet I am convinced, as are so many others, that the way in which our ordinary educational activities are carried out will not equip men with effective convictions. I would like to propose, in the light of what I have said about skill and intentionality, and to honor what I believe about the two faces of relevance, that there be a very basic change in pedagogical practice along the following lines.

First, education must no longer strike an exclusive posture of neutrality and objectivity. Knowledge, we know now as never before, is power. This does not mean that there are not canons of truth or that the idea of proof is not a precious one. Rather, let knowledge as it appears in our schooling be put into the context of action and commitment. The lawyer's brief, a parliamentary strategy, or a town planner's subtle balancings are as humanly important a way of knowing as a physicist's theorem. Gathering together the data for the indictment of a society that tolerates, in the United States, the ninth rank in infant mortality when it ranks first in gross national product— this is not an exercise in radical invective but in the mobilizing of knowledge in the interest of conviction that change is imperative. Let the skills of problem solving be given a chance to develop on problems that have an inherent passion—whether racism, crimes in the street, pollution, war and aggression, or marriage and the family.

Second, education must concentrate more on the unknown and the speculative, using the known and established as a basis for extrapolation. This will create two problems immediately. One is that the shift in emphasis will shake the traditional role of the teacher as the one who knows, contrasting with the student who does not. The other is that, in any body of men who use their minds at all, one usually gets a sharp division between what Joseph Agassis (1969) calls "knowers" and "seekers." Knowers are valuers of firm declarative statements about the state of things. Seekers regard such statements as invitations to speculation and doubt. The two groups often deplore each other. Just as surely as authority will not easily be given up by teachers, so too will knowers resist the threatening speculations of seekers. Revolution does have difficulties!

With respect to encouraging speculative extrapolation, I would particularly want to concentrate on "subjects" or "disciplines" that have a plainly visible growing edge, particularly the life sciences and the human sciences: human and behavioral biology, politics, economics, sociology, and psychology, organized around problems which have no clearly known solutions. The reward for working one's way through the known is to find a new question on the other side, formulated in a new way. Let it be plain that inquiry of this kind can be made not just through "the social sciences" but equally via the arts, literature, and philosophy, as well as by the syntactical sciences of logic and mathematical analysis.

Third, share the process of education with the learner. There are few things so exciting as sensing where one is trying to go, what one is trying to get hold of, and then making progress toward it. The reward of mastering something is the mastery, not the assurance that some day you will make more money or have more prestige. There must be a system of counseling that assures better than now that the learner knows what he is up to and that he has some hand in choosing the goal. This may be raising the spectre problem of totally individualized instruction. But learning *is* individual, no matter how many pupils there are per teacher. I am only urging that in the organization of curricula, units, and lessons, there be option provided as to how a student sets his goal for learning.

Fourth and finally, I would like to propose that as a transition we divide the curriculum into a Monday-Wednesday-Friday section that continues during the transition to work with what has been best in our school curricula up to this point, and a Tuesday-Thursday curriculum that is as experimental as we care to make it—seminars, political analyses, the development of position papers on school problems, "problem-finding" in the local community, you name it. Let it be as controversial as needs be. We are lacking diversity in experiment and can afford controversy in order to get it. Tuesday and Thursday need be no respecter of conventional teaching qualification. Indeed, it might provide the proper occasion for bringing outsiders into the school and "hooking" them with its challenge. I would also want to bring to the school—other than the conventional media of learning—film, political debate, and the carrying out of plans of action, all to be subject to scrutiny, discussion and criticism.

I am no innocent to matters of schooling and the conduct of instructional enterprises. What I am proposing involves a vast change in our thinking about schools, about growth, about the assumption of responsibility in the technological world as we know it. I have wanted to highlight the role of intention and goal directedness in learning and the acquisition of knowledge, and the conversion of skill into the management of one's own enterprises. The objective is to produce skill in our citizens, skill in the achieving of goals of personal significance, and of assuring a society in which personal significance can still be possible.

8

The Psychobiology
of Pedagogy

"Instruction" is, of course, a specialized artifact of human culture. It reflects the species-typical character of human culture and the requirement of passing on that culture by extragenetic means. If one takes culture to be a result of reflection of human biological characteristics, then "instruction" must also be thought of as constrained by the nature of a nervous system that is specialized for culture use. Is there some sense in which principles of pedagogy can be derived from our knowledge of man as a species—from knowledge of his characteristic growth and dependence, of the properties of his nervous system, of his modes of dealing with culture?

Three issues seem at the center of such an inquiry. The first has to do with the unique ways in which human development is culturally assisted in contrast to the means of assistance other species provide their young. This in turn leads to an examination of the devices a human culture provides its participants to amplify and extend their powers and how it transmits these from generation to generation. Then finally I will turn to some inherent constraints of the human nervous system better to appreciate opportunities and limitations of educability. I shall leave out of account, save to speculate upon it in passing, the very moot issue of whether the individual is the proper and sole focus of education, or whether the focus is some larger subgroup of the species. It is as important as any problem in education. For it is evident that once there is division of labor within a society, it is no longer isolated individual skill that is to be nurtured in isolation, but rather some orchestration of skills within a human group that needs joint cultivation. At the end, after discussing the other problems I shall return to this one.

The first point to be borne in mind about human development, in contrast to development elsewhere in the primate order, is the extent to which it is from the outside in as much as from the inside out. Two phenomena make this abundantly clear. The first is the role of language and other forms of symbolism, mastery of which endows the species with powers crucially beyond those attainable without such aids. Language, mathematics, or other theoretical ways of structuring knowledge capitalize upon innate capacities. But these skills, though they depend on innate capacities, originate *outside* the organism and memorialize generations of encounters by members of the culture. Use of the "outside-in" mode of development in the human species depends upon imitation and modeling. It is true that chimpanzees (for example, Goodall, 1965) and even Japanese macaques (Itami, 1958; Kawamura, 1959) show signs of "cultural transmission." But it obviously reaches critical mass, so to speak, only in man.

The evolutionary step that precipitated man's capacity for utilizing external culture and technology may always remain conjectural. Dart (1960), Washburn and Howell (1960), Le Gros Clark (1959), and others have begun to reconstruct the complex picture, of which we can mention only a few points here. More likely than not, the evolutionary trend toward the use of tools, culture, and associated traits among primates accelerated with the first emergence of bipedalism and the very primitive technical-social pattern of life that followed. When bipedalism freed the hands from locomotor function, some simple but adaptive tool using probably went with it. Given a process of selection of a primitive but effective tool user, there would also be concurrent selection of such traits as a bigger brain and a brain case expanded by reduction of the powerful jaw and supporting ridges in the skull. It may be proposed still further that selection of such a lighter skulled, less acromegalic variant of a species usually favors more docile traits, wildness being associated with bigger superorbital ridges and more prognathous jaws in higher mammals. Finally, it may well be the case that bipedalism also led to a strengthening of the supportive pelvic girdle by a closing down of its central aperture or birth canal. One may conjecture that if larger brained variants were being selected by environmental conditions, and had to pass through a smaller birth canal, an obvious compromise solution was the immature human brain, which grows from an initial 330 cc. capacity to about 1200 cc. Humans are born with less than one-quarter of eventual brain volume in contrast to close to three-quarters for macaques and gibbons. As Washburn remarks (1951), without culture and tools man would be among the "ecologically unimportant primates," and Oakley (1960) insists even more strongly that without compensating cultural factors, bipedalism in the open grassland and savannahs where it first occurs would be biologically disadvantageous. And Washburn (1968) puts a further point succinctly:

> Ecology has been stressed as an important factor in the origin of tool using. I would stress the social environment and the evolution of a social system in which skillful object use was rewarded. For example, in cultures where spear throwing is important, children practice this art in play. The children see the importance of the act in their parents' lives, and throughout the extended childhood of man, throwing is practiced with adult encouragement. Laughlin [1968] has described how Aleut children must be taught and must practice from early

childhood in order to be able to spear from a kayak. In non-human primates the absence of training and social reward means that the tool-using potential is never achieved. As Le Gros Clark [1967] has pointed out, chimpanzees can be trained to perform tasks that are beyond their unaided capacities; in other words, a human brain can guide chimpanzee practice and reward it to develop a new skill, but without human perception, training, and reward, the chimpanzee's performance is limited by both its biology and its social system.

Whether this reconstruction of origins is correct or not, the result of the process was to produce a species with less built-in behavioral determination, more docility, and more reliance on external sources of skill and knowledge made possible by a capacity for symbolic activity. A new phase in organic evolution begins in which pedagogy takes on increasing significance as the DNA code decreases in the specificity of its instructions. Professor Edmund Leach (1968) makes much of man taking on the role of God. One could not possibly make the point strongly enough. Man not only creates his own environment, but in so doing eventually presides over the programming and realization of his own evolution—however inadvertent and stumbling he may be about it.

It is in the light of these considerations that one must view the system used for passing on the corpus of human skills enshrined in the culture to a next generation, a corpus of skills ranging widely from technology to ways of reckoning and ways of representing manageably the recurrent regularities of the environment, to myth making, and many others.

To begin with, virtually all powerful human skills involve the mastery of a series of prerequisites. One learns something in order to learn something next. One major function of human pedagogy is to develop and provide means that allow a learner swiftly and surely to run through various prerequisite series and thus to achieve a full and early use of the culture and its technology. But the construction of prerequisites presents difficulties. For one thing, the steps of instruction must match the child's own trends of growth. For another, the learner must be brought to independence at the end of the sequence rather than becoming perennially dependent on outside instruction. Yet for all that, once skill is achieved, interest in further learning and further exploitation of achieved skills must be kept alive. How one manages to time the steps in pedagogy to match unfolding capacities, how one manages to instruct without making the learner dependent, and how one manages to do both of these while keeping alive zest for further learning—these are very complicated questions that do not yield easy answers.

With respect to matching successive prerequisites to the "natural" limits of developing intellectual skills, most work suggests that it is often best done first through embodiment of principles in action, then by the supplement of image, and finally in symbolic form. Whether one is teaching set theory, the conservation of momentum and inertia, or the notion of representation before the law, one does well to begin with concrete actions to be performed, passing on to a vivid case or paradigm instance, and coming finally to the formal description in natural language or mathematics. It has been true of various curriculum projects that their success depended upon the invention of appropriate embodiments of ideas in these three modes—in action, image, and symbol. The balance beam, the pendulum, the proper set of modular blocks, the well-designed game or role play, the right vivarium or culture of growing yeast cells, the study of the proper tribal group—these may be high technological achievements in education. In time, one visits and revisits the same general principles, rendering them increasingly more abstract and formal, more precise, more powerful, more generative. It is a point made many times in many guises in these essays.

With respect to making accessible the deep structure of any given discipline, I think the rule still holds that any subject can be taught to any child at any age in some form that is both honest and powerful. It is a premise that rests on the fact that more complex abstract ideas can in fact be rendered in an intuitive, operational form that comes within reach of any learner to aid him toward the more abstract idea yet to be mastered. One can, in short, become alert and deft about using the mind, the eye, and the hand for a variety of purposes.

Knowledge has a structure, a hierarchy, in which some of

what is known is more significant than the rest of what is known about some aspect of life or nature. It is more significant because armed with the significant knowledge and armed with a theory and operations for putting the significant knowledge together and for going beyond it, one can reconstruct with reasonable approximation the less significant knowledge and the multitude of stray items that constitute the whole body of knowledge. The task of the curriculum maker and of teachers is to give to the student a grasp of this underlying structure along with a highly discriminating sense of its importance so that he may be saved from that most common blight on human thinking: clutter.

This view argues against charity toward irrelevant detail. It is not harmless. It is lethal. For it can be said about our knowledge of knowledge that very little of it can be dealt with by the human mind at one time. The range of human attention is highly limited, we now know by comparing men and machines. But this is both its strength and its weakness. It imposes a need for economy in man as to what it is that he bears in mind. It is this that makes theory a necessity rather than a luxury. A concept or the connected body of concepts that is a theory is man's only means of getting a lot into the narrow compass of his attention all at a time. Without some such aid, there is clutter.

The knowledge explosion, to be sure, is something of a hoax. From outside it looks like an explosion. From inside it seems more like an implosion. For not only is there ever more of it around—the exploding part—but it turns out on closer inspection that it is all more interconnected than ever before suspected. Another way of saying it is that though there are many more facts, there are far more powerful theories with which to reduce or implode them to an order that can be understood.

As for helping the human learner achieve a mastery of his own without ending up dependent on the sources from which he has learned, I suspect that the answer is twofold. On the one hand, there is the cultivation of a sense of autonomy and competence in the broadest personal sense, and here the issue is whether the culture fosters such a sense of effectiveness within the individual. But more than that, there is a question of whether what the individual has learned equips him to generate knowledge and opinions on his own. Insofar as knowledge is treated as inert, as revealed, as providing no base for "going beyond the information given" (see Bruner, 1957), then confidence and autonomy will not substitute for intellectual competence. Imagine then, a child raised in an atmosphere of hopelessness and passivity, whose view of impersonal knowledge is that it is arbitrary and happenstantial, and you have a description of the dependent—either of the defeated or of the reactively destructive antagonist whose only way of escaping from defeat is to destroy the system that assured defeat.

The activation of interest and the motivation to learn is a dark subject. The simple view of it is that you provide reinforcement for a response, and the response will be learned. Let me assure you that reinforcement is anything but an obvious phenomenon. Even if a principle of reinforcement held, there would be a question of competition among reinforcements from different sources. What gets reinforced by whom? And it obscures the issue to talk of intellectual learning as if it consisted of some linear sequence of reinforceable responses. In the end, motivation is exceedingly difficult to control, particularly where the acquisition of the prerequisites of knowledge or skill is concerned.

Yet it is plain enough that the process of being educated must appear to the learner to have some eventual value for him, that he values the achievement of competence in "school subjects." Knowledge and skill may themselves be highly rewarding. But unless the individual has some sense of their leading to something beyond themselves, I suspect there will be erosion even of these pleasures. What must knowledge and skill lead to?

I would prefer to look at the matter in terms of Lévi-Strauss's (1963) conception of the reciprocal patterns of human culture. He proposes that the three basic scarce commodities of exchange are symbolically coded information, affiliation, and goods and services—a semiotic system, a kinship system, and an economic-technological system. Full participation in a culture involves not only being enmeshed in these systems (which one inevitably is) but having a sense of some appropriate equity in them. It is this sense of equity that stimulates a drive to master the culturally relevant skills. Education as a process must be seen by the learner as relevant to achieving that equity. But once education is removed from the context of action, as it is when put into a school, the relevance of education to one's feeling of equity becomes more difficult to see. And indeed, once a youth culture develops that is isolated from the society at large, the necessarily step-by-step mastery of skills becomes the more galling. And in time, the process of education comes to seem burdensome and the results become, in fact, unrewarding.

With this much of an introduction, we turn to the issue with which we began—what are the constraints placed on the educational process by the nature of a human nervous system operating with the aid of human culture?

CONSTRAINTS ON EDUCATION

The first constraint is a severe one. The human nervous system, like any other nervous system, is severely limited in the amount of information it can process at any one time. There is a distinction between monitoring and processing. A clerk working for a clipping service can scan papers for the names of up to twenty-five customers at a time, and even more prodigious feats of parallel processing can be brought off (for example, Shepard, 1967)—provided no further processing than identification is involved. Once the task goes beyond "spotting," the severe limits of focal attention come into play. There are several interesting reasons for these limits—fast fading, interference, retrieval problems, the bottleneck limitations of a final common path—which need not concern us here except that we must note that they cannot be overcome directly either by tricks or by training.

Given such limits, it becomes necessary for the learner to reduce the strain and potential confusion of receiving and processing input. He does so by developing strategies for using his limited capacities. This type of strategic learning is characteristic of every level of information handling—from eye-movements (Mackworth and Bruner, 1970), through perceptual structuring (Neisser, 1967), to thought and problem solving (Bruner, Goodnow, and Austin, 1956; Newell, Shaw, and Simon, 1958). The strategies, at whatever level, have a few crucial features in common:

i.   We are selective; we attend to some things, not to others.
ii. We are economical for the sake of speed and strain re-duction, we utilize minimal cues and do not linger with information in reaching decisions.
iii. We are sensitive to steady properties. The minimal cues eventually selected are the invariant features of things attended to.
iv. We are connective. Invariant features are put together as working models, as configurations, as causes-and-effects.
v.   We are alarmed by deviance. We have special alarm mechanisms for events that deviate beyond a certain amount from our models.
vi. We are extrapolative. We easily go beyond the information given by processes of inference that come as naturally as breathing.

You will have noted that a limited nervous system has strategies that make and use theories in the usual sense—find-ing ways of dealing with a great deal of information while keeping very little in mind. Note too that such theory has the property of being exemplified by doing, by depiction in an image, or by restatement in words. Theories, models, myths, cause-and-effect accounts, ways of looking and seeing as well as ways of thinking are probably *the* prime prosthetic device for assisting nervous systems beyond their naked limits. To paraphrase George Miller (1956), they provide a way of filling the limited slots of attention, memory, and thought with gold rather than dross. So theories—the term may be too grand but I would prefer to give the human nervous system the benefit of doubt—theories quickly become the valued property of a cul-ture, constantly undergoing revision and often refinement to-ward greater abstraction as they find more compact restatement in the arts and in myth as well as in the formalism of science.

One obvious implication of this view of strategies of knowing is that "experience" is relative to the code in terms of which it was interpreted; it is never had neat and neutral. This is commonplace, of course, in the philosophy of science since Mach (1914), but it is an issue often neglected in discussions of education save in attacks on relativism. In fact, we overcome relativism by the invention of techniques of calibration that provide a workable basis of dealing with events communally— techniques of inference, techniques for testing hypotheses, for sampling, for locating and correcting inconsistency and contradiction, and so on. They provide safeguards against the kind of error-proneness that is inherent in human nervous systems. They are the techniques, alas, that come under the gun of the anti-intellectuals to whom commitment outweighs proof.

A closely related rule about pedagogy derives from the work of von Holst and Mittelstaedt (1950), Bernstein (1967), Held and Hein (1958), and others. In its roughest form, it is the generalization that sensory input into a system is related to the action on which it impinges. Identical movements of the hand— one produced by a bar shaking the hand, the other produced by the hand shaking the bar—are differently interpreted.

I would wish to argue that the principle has its homologue in the higher nervous system as well. It takes the form in ordinary experience of data being interpretable only in the light of the hypothesis one brings to bear upon it. This is essentially the "hypothesis" theory of perception (see Bruner, 1951; F. H. Allport, 1961) whose central premise is that it is the *processing* of data that yields significance, not its *receipt*. There is always a matching that must occur between the input of data and one's expectation or hypothesis.

One implication of this for pedagogical practice is that instruction must encourage the formulation and testing of hypotheses. One of the most successful experiments in contemporary pedagogy has been conducted by Covington, Crutchfield, and Davies (1966) at Berkeley. They used a comicstrip series, featuring a physics teacher (who moonlights as a private detective) and his nephew and niece who help him in his crime detection. One series has as its aim to encourage the children to pause and predict who is the guilty party on the basis of admittedly insufficient information. The game works not only in improving performance on similar games of inference, but also on performance in school subjects from social studies to mathematics. I shall say no more about this principle, for the idea of deriving hypotheses and of giving training in doing so is so implicit in what has already been said about theory as a prosthetic device.

Another constraint imposed by human neural functioning has to do with its management of complexity. Infancy provides good examples. If we present a month-old baby sucking the nipple of a bottle with a moving object that catches the infant's eyes and produces ocular convergence, the sucking stops in mid-career. Later, when nutritive sucking is organized into well-modularized bursts and pauses, a new principle of inter-calation between sucking and looking begins. The infant shuts down attention during sucking bursts and opens up during pauses. The first form of behavioral integration, dominated by *suppression,* is now replaced by a system regulated by orderly *succession.*

Still later, toward four months, another rule comes to prevail. Sucking, you may know, can be divided into a rhythmic mouth-ing component and a suction component. The presentation of a lively visual stimulus to the more developed four-month-old is likely to make the baby stop sucking, but he continues mouth-ing rhythmically as a "place-holding" activity that brings him back to his feeding after a more prolonged look at the engag-ing object. Such place-holding opens a new range of options for coordinating action in different domains. And for complex activity to be brought off intelligently, it must have a sequential pattern such that the whole is kept in mind while the parts are strung together—as with the syntactical structure of the sen-tence in ordinary language. For the infant, from then on, vir-tually all skilled activity is regulated in this way: What this means, in effect, is that there is a plan "in the mind" of the per-son acting that is prior to and in control of the sequential or serial idea of events.

Curiously enough, though this is a crucial problem in man-aging what Herbert Simon (1962) has called the "architecture of complexity," there is very little account taken of it in organiz-ing the lessons of the young. Was "home work" originally in-tended for the cultivation of self-initiated planning of one's intellectual effort? Generally, pedagogy is grossly unmindful of the serial order of virtually all problem solving and does little to encourage having a plan in mind that is prior to and controlling a sequence of events.

This brings me to my final constraint, and it is one that relates to our earlier discussion of skill and knowledge depending upon prerequisite learning. I wish to consider briefly some very early prerequisites. There seems to be little evidence, let me say at the outset, for anything like critical periods in human growth—such that, for example, if a skill is not learned during a particular period in the life cycle, it cannot be learned later. The only exception may be in the sphere of language: we do not know whether language can be learned after a certain age, though we do know that if a particular language is *not* learned by ten or eleven, its phonology will never be fully mastered in the manner of a native speaker. But what does seem evident, even if there are not dramatic, all-or-none watershed points in human development, is that certain skills *not* learned early come much harder later. It is not plain whether this is in the nature of the skill itself or a function of a compensatory skill that develops to provide a fail-safe backup for the original lack—as with some late-operated cataract cases who develop so strong a dependence on the protective strategies of the blind that they have great difficulty in adopting sight as a guide when vision is restored (for example, Gregory, 1966).

We are usually accustomed these days to think of the role of early learning from the point of view of "the disadvantaged" or "the culturally deprived child." Working with normal infancy, I find this emphasis short-sighted. For the abiding fact of all human immaturity is its openness to attentional, cognitive, affective, social, and linguistic cultivation. I would urge that we begin our inquiry into the bases of a species-specific pedagogy with a much closer look at the opportunities provided in early immaturity for the cultivation of highly generic skills. Better to illustrate, let me give a few examples from work in the laboratory at Harvard. My colleagues and I have been much concerned with how infants begin to build a model or theory of their environment in order to anticipate events with more lead time. The experiments (for example, Bruner, 1969) need not concern us in any detail. The one point I would want to make about a good many of them relates to the deployment of attention in infancy in the interest both of anticipating familiar events and in foreseeing the possibility of novelty. Thus, in one experiment conducted by Mundy-Castle and Anglin (1969), infants from ten days to five months of age are presented with vivid visual objects, appearing in regular succession now in one window before them, now in the other. Soon they learn to look where the action is, at the windows; then to fasten undeviatingly upon each object when it appears, leaving it only at its disappearance to fasten on the other; finally, they come to observe one object, though monitoring the other locus with quick but not frequent fast eye movements to see whether anything else is going on there. It is not so much the achievement of this rather paltry though important anticipatory skill that concerns me here, but rather the general nature of the infant's reaction to its mastery.

For one thing, infants will stay at this task for a long time— they are absorbed by it. Their alertness is striking, with notable continuation of the orienting response of the eyes. One notices also, in several experiments, that there are signs of pleasure in prediction. My associate Hanus Papousek (1967) at Prague has photographed infants in the third and fourth month smiling when they have learned to predict the side on which a feeding nipple will appear on the basis of a signal tone preceding it— smiling rather than taking the nipple. We have seen the same thing (Kalnins, 1970), indeed, in our own laboratory when an infant learns how, by sucking above a certain rate on a blind nipple, to bring a motion picture into focus, an experiment discussed more fully in the next chapter.

This suggests to me that there may be a time in development—judging by interest and signs of pleasure—when infants should be given an opportunity to exercise and cultivate certain functions. I cannot say whether it makes a difference in their later growth, simply because the research has not been done. But I would be negligent if I did not bring to attention this possibility. I realize too that there is evidence that indicates, as with Myrtle McGraw's (1935) famous twin study of a generation ago, that the child started later soon catches up. But these studies have two restrictions that bring them into question. The first is that they were mainly concerned with motor activity, usually related to the full realization of bipedalism, for which there is a natural and a social push already in existence. But much more seriously, they are "one-shot" episodes. One child is taught to skate or ride a bicycle as early as he can manage, the twin waits till later. He catches up within some months or at most a year. But what if a first skill mastered is now used to master a second skill to which it is prerequisite? And then to a next skill? I do not mean to make it sound as if childhood should be a grim parade toward the achievement of early skills. I urge only that we not turn a blind eye to the possibility that the achievement of the full human potential is dependent upon the use of more than common ingenuity in the care of the very young. Indeed, it is a strange species, *Homo sapiens,* that has not explored the outline of a theory of toys though so many of us know that the childhood of its members is obviously prolonged with some good biological purpose.

Let me conclude with a point that I have perhaps made too often already. Man is not a naked ape but a culture-clothed human being, hopelessly ineffective without the prosthesis provided by culture. The very nature of his characteristics as a species provides a guide to appropriate pedagogy, and the nature of his nervous system and its constraints provides a basis for devising reasonable if not inevitable principles for designing a testable pedagogy. I have no particular warrant to assert that the few properties of neural functioning we have considered are *the* crucial ones to consider, nor that the conclusions I have drawn are anything more than reasonable. But my object is *not* to establish exhaustive principles so much as to urge that it is by exercises such as this one that the need for principles be established.

9

Poverty
and Childhood

I should like to consider what psychologists know about the education of the very young, about influences during infancy and early childhood that may be formative upon later intellectual competence, and how these influences may be more compassionately deployed. The focus will be upon the manner in which social and cultural background affects upbringing and thereby affects intellectual functioning. Within that wide compass, I shall limit myself further by concentrating principally upon the impact of poverty and dispossession.

There is little enough systematic knowledge about what in fact happens to children during infancy and early childhood and even less on what its latter effects on competence may be. Indeed, in the current debates, it is a moot point as to what is properly meant by intellectual competence, whether or in what degree competence comprises soul, mind, heart, or the general community. Nor can the topic be limited to education. For the charge has been made by Royal Commissions and advisers to Presidents as well as by the anti-Establishment New Left that educational and socializing practice, before the school years as after, reflects and reinforces the inequities of a class system. This it does by limiting access to knowledge for the poor while facilitating it for those better off. The charge is even more serious: that our practice of education, both in and out of school, assures uneven distribution not only of knowledge but also of competence to profit from knowledge. It does so by limiting and starving the capabilities of the children of the poor by leading them into failure until they are convinced that it is not worth their while to think about school-like things. As Stodolsky and Lesser (1967) grimly put it, "When intelligence data and early achievement data are combined we have a predictor's paradise, but an abysmal prognosis for most children who enter the school system from disadvantaged backgrounds."

Why concentrate on the very young? The answer is, of course, in the form of a wager. For one thing, Bloom's (1964) careful and well-known work strongly suggests that a very major proportion of the variance in adult intellectual achievement, measured by a wide variety of procedures, is already accounted for by the time the child reaches the usual school-starting age of five. For another, there are enough studies to indicate, as we shall see, that certain possibly critical emotional, linguistic, and cognitive patterns associated with social background are already present by age three. But principally, I am moved to concentrate on the very young by my own research (for example, Bruner, 1969; Bruner, Lyons, and Kaye, 1971). The staggering rate at which the preschool child acquires skills, expectancies, and notions about the world and about people; the degree to which culturally specialized attitudes shape the care of children during these years—these are impressive matters that lend concreteness to the official manifestos about the early years.

Our first task is to examine what is known about the effects of poverty on child development in our contemporary Western culture—whether this knowledge comes from attempted intervention, from naturalistic studies, or from the laboratory. I do not wish to make a special issue of poverty, of whether or not it represents a self-sustaining culture, as Oscar Lewis (1966) urges; nor do I want to make the claim that poverty is in every culture the same. Yet there are common elements that are crucial wherever it is encountered and in whatever culture imbedded. I shall have more to say about these in context as we consider what it is that poverty and its attendant sense of powerlessness may do to the pattern of growth in children.

The second task is to look briefly at modern theories of development with a view to assessing whether they aid in the understanding of the impact of culture on growth, generally, and of the impact of poverty, particularly.

Finally, and again too briefly, we must examine what the implications of this exercise are for public policy and for the conduct of early education. As Robert Hess (1968) puts it, "The current growth of programs in early education and the large-scale involvement of the schools and federal government in them is not a transitory concern. It represents a fundamental shift in the relative roles and potential influence of the two major socializing institutions of the society—the family and the school."

Most of the work that compares children from different socioeconomic backgrounds points to three interconnected influences associated with poverty. The first relates to the opportunity for, the encouragement of, and the management of goal seeking and of problem solving; it reflects differences in the degree to which one feels powerless or powerful, and in the realistic expectation of reward for effort. *What* the child strives for, *how* he goes about the task of means-end analysis, his expectations of success and failure, his approach to the *delay* of gratification, his *pacing* of goal setting—these are not only crucial but they also affect how he uses language, deploys attention, processes information, and so on. The second influence is linguistic: by exposure to many situations and through the application of many demands, children come to *use* language in different ways, particularly as an instrument of thought, of social control and interaction, of planning, and the like. The third influence comes from the pattern of reciprocity into which the child moves, whether middle class or poor and dispossessed. What parents expect, what teachers demand, what peers anticipate—all of these operate to shape outlook and approach in the young. We must consider each of these in turn.

GOAL SEEKING AND PROBLEM SOLVING

A close reading of the evidence surely suggests that the major source of "cognitive" difference between poor and better off, between those who feel powerless and those who feel less so, lies in the different way goals are defined and how means to their attainment are fashioned and brought into play.

Begin with a general proposition: that one feels competent about oneself before feeling competent about others or about the world at large. Moffett (1968) observes how language complexity increases when the child writes or speaks about events in which the child himself has participated in a goal-seeking process. Consider these unlikely initial subordinate constructions from third-graders uttered in describing a task in which they have had a central, directive role:

> *If I place a flame over the candle,*
> *the candle goes out.*
> *When you throw alum on the candle,*
> *the flame turns blue.*

Or take two speech samples from lower-class black children, one describing a TV episode in "The Man From U.N.C.L.E.," the other a fight in which he, the speaker, was engaged.

> *This kid—Napoleon got shot*
> *And he had to go on a mission*
> *And so this kid, he went with Solo.*
> *So they went.*
> *And this guy—they went through this window.*
> *And they caught him.*

> *And they beat-up them other people.*
> *And they went*
> *and then he said that this*
> *old lady was his mother*
> *and then he—and at the end he say*
> *that he was the guy's friend.*

And the fight:

> When I was in the fourth grade—
> no it was in the third grade—
> This boy he stole my glove.
> He took my glove
> and said that his father found it downtown
>   on the ground.
> (And you fight him?)
> I told him that it was impossible for him
>   to find downtown 'cause all those people
>   was walking by and just his father
>   was the only one that found it?
> So he got all (mad).
> So then I fought him.
> I knocked him all out in the street.
> So he say he give
> and I kept on hitting him.
> Then he started crying
> and ran home to his father
> And the father told him
> that he didn't find no glove.

As Labov (1969) remarks, the difference between the two is that the second has a consistent evaluative perspective or narrative line, from the speaker to the events that impinge upon him, and back to his reactions to these events.

A study by Strandberg and Griffith (1968) provides the third example. Four- and five-year-olds were given Kodak Instamatic cameras and told to take any pictures that interested them. Their subsequent utterances about these pictures were compared with what they said of comparable pictures that they had photographed when told to do so in order to learn. In the first of the two excerpts, the child struggles—unsuccessfully —to find a context for an assigned picture. In the second, describing one he took on his own, it is built in. The speaker is a five-year-old.

> *That's a horse. You can ride it. I don't*
> *know any more about it. It's brown, black,*
> *and red. I don't know my story about the horse.*
> *There's a picture of my tree that I climb in.*
> *There's—there's where it grows at and there's*
> *where I climb up—and sit up there—*
> *down there and that's where I look out at.*
> *First I get on this one and then I get on that*
> *other one. And then I put my foot under*
> *that big branch that are so strong. And*
> *then I pull my face up and when I get*
> *a hold of a branch up at that place—and*
> *then I look around.*

The bare, schoolish organization of the first seems so detached next to the intentional, active, egocentric perspective of the second.

Shift now, without benefit of transition, to much younger children, infants of four to six weeks being studied at the Center for Cognitive Studies. In this study, conducted by Kalnins (1970), infants control the focus of a lively motion picture by sucking at a present rate on a special nipple. In one condition, sucking at or faster than the prescribed rate brings the moving picture into focus and keeps it there. In the other, sucking at this rate drives the picture out of focus and keeps it out. One group of infants starts with sucking for clarity and shifts to the suck-for-blur condition. The other begins with the suck-for-blur and shifts to the suck-for-clear condition—though the two conditions are never presented in the same session, or, indeed, on the same visit to the Center. Note two crucial points about performance. The first is that the infants respond immediately and appropriately to the consequences produced by their sucking—the pauses averaging about four seconds in suck-for-clear and about eight seconds in suck-for-blur. As soon as the consequences of sucking alters, the infant's response pattern shifts abruptly and appropriately. As a further feature of reacting to consequences in both conditions, the infant averts his gaze from the picture when it is out of focus—while sucking in the case of suck-for-blur, and while pausing in the other case.

For those not acquainted with the data on infant learning, these findings may seem a trifle bizarre though otherwise quite to be expected. They are, in fact, rather unexpected in the immediacy of the learning reported, particularly in the light of the painfully slow process of *classical* conditioning found in infants of comparable age by Papousek (1967), Lipsett (1967) and others. Papousek's infants turned their head one way or another *in response* to an environmental event, as did the babies in the Brown University experiments. Kalnins' babies were learning to respond not to a stimulus, *but to a change produced by their own act,* and to store the information thus gained as an instrumental sequence involving their own action. Indeed, it may well be that a special type of recurring "critical period" is to be found in the few thousand milliseconds that follow upon a voluntarily initiated act. This is not the proper context in which to treat the matter in detail, yet it must be said emphatically that since the pioneer work of von Holst and Mittelstaedt (1950), the role of intention has become increasingly central in biology and psychology.

It was Held and Hein (1958) who first showed how crucial the reafference output of "intentional" movement was for adaptation learning. In their now famous experiment with yoked kittens adapting to prismatically induced angular displacement in the visual field, one kitten actively walked about an environment, the other was passively transported in a gondola through an identical path. The former adapted to the prisms, the latter did not. While we are still far from understanding the neural mechanisms of intentionality—variously called reafference, feed-forward, motor-to-sensory mechanism corrolary discharge, or "Sollwert"—there are a sufficient number of leads to suggest that the pursuit will pay off.

In a word, probably the first type of acquired representation of the world the child achieves is in the form of an egocentrically oriented action schema: a joint representation of action intended along with the consequences of that action, a matter to which Piaget (1954) has devoted some of his most exquisite descriptions.

But if one thinks of acquired egocentric orientation only as a phase out of which the child must grow en route to becoming operational and decentered, then a crucial point may be overlooked. In Vygotsky's (1962) terms, the stream of action and the stream of language begin to converge in the process of interacting with the world in just such an egocentric orientation.

My colleague Dr. Greenfield (1969) notes, "Not only can people fail to realize goals, the environment can fail to provide a growth-promoting sequence for them. I should like to suggest that the goals set for the child by his caretakers and the relation of these to the child's available means is a critical factor in determining the rate and richness of cognitive growth in the early, formative years." She goes on to comment in this context, "If a mother believes her fate is controlled by external forces, that she does not control the means necessary to achieve her goals, what does this mean for her children?" The follow-up data from the Hess (1969) group's study of the relation between maternal variables and the development of intelligence (to which we shall turn shortly) show that the more a mother feels externally controlled when her child is four years old, the more likely the child is to have a low IQ and a poor academic record at age six or seven.

Striking documentation of these points is beginning to be available at the intimate level of family interaction. One such study, now in progress, is Maxine Schoggen's (1969), an effort to elucidate differences in directed action that had been found in the children of the five-year study of Klaus and Gray (1968). She uses an "environmental force unit" or EFU, which is defined as an act by any social agent in the child's environment directed toward getting the child to seek a goal. One crude finding already available—the data are only now in process of analysis—is that, for lower-class families, some two-thirds of the children are below the total median rate for EFUs per minute, whereas only a quarter of the middle income children are. This suggests how great a difference there may be in sheer emphasis upon goal directedness in the two groups.

One must note also that in the two major studies of how middle-class and poverty mothers instruct their children—Hess and Shipman (1965); and Bee, et al. (1969)—a quite comparable trend emerged. They found, first, that middle-class mothers are more attentive to the continuous flow of goal-directed action. Second, they allow the child to set his own pace and make his own decisions more. Third, they intrude less often and less directly in the process of problem solving itself. Fourth, they structure the search task by questions that sharpen yet ease the search for means. Fifth, they are more oriented toward the overall structure of the task than responsive to component acts in isolation. Sixth, they react more to the child's successful efforts than to his errors (a practice far more likely to evoke further verbal interaction between tutor and child). These surely suggest some of the crucial differences that emerge in the goal-seeking patterns of economically advantaged and disadvantaged children.

To this evidence must now be added findings from still another type of research, longer-term longitudinal studies tracing human growth from infancy through adolescence.

Kagan and Moss (1964) state in their well-known monograph, "It appears that the pattern most likely to lead to involvement in intellectual achievement in the boys is early maternal protection, followed by encouragement and acceleration of mastery behaviors." And then, "Following our best judgment in estimating the most desirable patterns to follow with young children, our educated guess remains that higher intelligence is fostered by warmth, support, and plentiful opportunity and reward for achievement and autonomy. Moreover, it is probably important to provide active, warm, achievement-oriented parental figures of both sexes after whom appropriate role patterns can be established." Add to this, finally, the conclusion reached by Robinson and Robinson (1968) in their review: "Children with a high degree of achievement motivation tend to become brighter as they grow older; those with a more passive outlook tend to fall behind their developmental potential (Bayley and Schaefer, 1964; Sontag, Baker, and Nelson, 1958). The degree of achievement motivation is related to the socio-cultural background of the child; middle-class children are more strongly motivated toward achievement than are lower-class children (Douvan, 1956; Lott and Lott, 1963; Mussen, Urbano and Bouterline-Young, 1961)."

There is a further multiplier factor in the effects we have been discussing: the impact of urbanization on the care of children. We have, until now, argued that poverty, by its production of a sense of powerlessness, alters goal striving and problem solving in those it affects, whether the powerlessness occurs in a depressed London working-class borough, among Kurdistani immigrants to Israel, in a black ghetto, among uneducated and abandoned Greenland Eskimo mothers down-and-out in literate Copenhagen, or in the midst of Appalachia. The evidence points to a magnification of this effect when poverty moves to the city. Perhaps the most comprehensive study to date is by Graves (1969), who has compared rural and urban Spanish Americans around Denver, as well as rural and urban Baganda around Kampala and Entebbe in Uganda. Interviews with mothers in her study show that urban mothers come to believe more than rural mothers that their preschool children cannot understand, cannot be taught ideas or skills, cannot be depended on. City mothers rated their children lower in potentialities for independence, for self-reliance, and for ability to help with the family. It is a cycle. When the poor mother moves to the city, she becomes trapped with her children—more irritable, more interested in keeping peace than in explaining and encouraging adventure. She often, then, produces the very behavior she rates down. The urban environment itself restricts outlets for the child and, at the same time, reduces the mother's confidence in her children's capacity for coping with those that are left.

Warren Haggstrom (1964), in a masterful review of the literature on the effects of poverty, comes to the conclusion that "the fact of being powerless, but with needs that must be met, leads the poor to be dependent on the organizations, persons, and institutions which can meet these needs. The situation of dependency and powerlessness, through internal personality characteristics as well as through social position, leads to apathy, hopelessness, conviction of the inability to act successfully, failure to develop skills, and so on."

Consider now some consequences of this pattern on the development of language usage in interactive speech, and likely as well in the internal use of speech in problem solving.

LANGUAGE AND POVERTY

It was perhaps the studies of Hess and Shipman (1965), inspired by Basil Bernstein (1961), that drew attention to *how* language was used in communicating with young children and what its significance was to the lower- and the middle-class child. They asked mothers to instruct their own children to use an Etch-a-Sketch drawing pad, taking careful note of the mother's language and her mode of instruction. Their general conclusions have already been discussed. Looking in detail at linguistic considerations, we turn to a more recent study that used Hess and Shipman's system of classification with further elaboration. It documents the work carried out by Helen Bee and her colleagues (1969) at the University of Washington with four- to five-year-olds. The Washington group also asked the mother to help her child accomplish a task (copying a house of blocks); in addition they observed mother-child interaction in the well-supplied waiting room and interviewed the mother afterwards about her ideas on looking after children. An excerpt from their paper can serve as summary.

> The middle-class mother tended to allow her child to work at his own pace, offered many general structuring suggestions on how to search for the solution to a problem, and told the child what he was doing that was correct . . . The general structure offered by the mother may help the child acquire learning sets (strategies) which will generalize to future problem solving situations.
>
> In contrast, the lower-class mother did not behave in ways

which would encourage the child to attend to the basic features of the problem. Her suggestions were highly specific, did not emphasize basic problem-solving strategies, and seldom required a reply from the child. Indeed, she often deprived the child of the opportunity to solve the problem on his own by her non-verbal intrusions into the problem-solving activity.

They comment on the fact that middle-class mothers ask so many more questions in an effort to help the child in his task that their mode of operating linguistically could fairly be called "interrogative," in contrast to the more indicative and imperative modes of lower class mothers.

Hess and Shipman (1965) had, of course, found quite comparable differences in mothers, though they distinguished three modes of communicating: cognitive-rational, imperative-normative, and personal-subjective. In the first the mother was task-oriented, informative, and analytic; in the second, she ordered and evaluated; and in the third, she pleaded for performance on grounds that it would please her. The highest concentration of the first mode was found among middle-class mothers.

Both studies point to early class differences in language use. One is the use of language to dissect a problem. In lower-class discourse, mothers more often order, or plead, or complain, than set up a problem or give feedback. Such usage possibly accounts for the "poor reinforcement value" of verbal reactions by the parents of less advantaged children (see, for example, Zigler, 1968): language is not usually used for signaling outcome or hailing good tries. What is most lacking in the less-advantaged mother's use of language is analysis-and-synthesis: the dissection of relevant features in a task and their appropriate recombinations in terms of connection, cause-and-effect, and so on.

The evidence surely leads one to the conclusion that there is more demand for, as well as more use of, analytic language among middle-class than among lower-class speakers. Turner and Pickvance (1970), for example, attempted to measure the difference by counting incidences of uncertainty in the verbal expressions of sixteen-year-olds from middle-class and poverty backgrounds who were making up stories or interpreting uncertain events. "Orientation toward the use of expressions of uncertainty is more strongly related to social class than to verbal ability . . . In every case in which social class has been shown to be related to the use of expressions of uncertainty, it was the middle-class child who used more of them;" the middle-class child had more recourse to Wh- questions, to the use of "might be . . ." and "could be . . . ," to *I think*, and to refusals to commit himself. As the authors say, "Bernstein's work suggests that the forms of socialization typically employed in middle-class families are likely to give the children reared in these families greater scope for self-regulation, for operating within a wide range of alternatives. These socialization procedures . . . are likely to give these children a greater awareness of uncertainty in certain areas of experience and are likely to encourage the children to be flexible in their thinking."

Other evidence also suggests a difference in analytic discrimination. Klaus and Gray (1968), among impoverished black children in Murfreesboro, Tennessee, and Robinson and Creed (1968), with slum children in London's Borough of Newham, agree in finding less fine discriminations made by lower-class than by middle-class children—at least in rather impersonal, school-like tasks. Marion Blank (1969) shows that tutoring children from poverty backgrounds to extract features from displays—distance, direction, form, for example —increases their measured intelligence (long a belief of Maria Montessori). Indeed, it is not surprising that Earl Shaefer's (1969) careful intervention study with one- to three-year-old children in poverty families emphasizes such discriminative training, with good results in raising standard intelligence scores.

Another index of the analytic use of language is the accumulation of vocabulary. As Cazden (1970) puts it, "Consideration of vocabulary as an aspect of language cannot be separated from considerations of concepts as the whole of our personal knowledge. The content of our mental dictionary catalogs more than our knowledge of language; it catalogs our substantive knowledge of the world." Brown, Cazden, and Bellugi

(1969) also point out that most instances of natural language instruction between parent and child relate to word meanings —true not only in their small Cambridge sample, but also for two lower-class black mothers in a Great Lakes city (Horner, 1968) and for mothers in Samoa (Slobin, 1968). It is of special interest then that Coleman (1966) noted that vocabulary subtests of an IQ test were more correlated with differences in quality of schools than were achievement tests in such more formal school subjects as arithmetic and reading. This suggests that the push to analysis, differentiation, synthesis, and so on, is accompanied by a push to achieve economy of means of representation in words. Again, the more active the intellectual push of the environment, the more the differentiation of concepts and of words, their markers. Hence the richer, better stocked vocabulary of the middle-class child.

Perhaps the most telling example of increased analytic-synthetic activity in speech per se comes from Joan Tough's study of two groups of three-year-olds, matched for IQ and about equal in verbal output, one of middle-, the other of working-class background. Even at this age, middle-class children single out many more qualitative features of the environment to talk about, and indeed, also talk much more of such relations between them as cause-and-effect. So there is good reason to believe that there is an early start to the differentiating process whereby children from one social class move toward a program of linguistic analysis-and-synthesis while the others move toward something else. Klaus and Gray (1968) remark on this "something else": "the children with whom we worked tended to have little categorizing ability except in affective terms; they were highly concrete and immediate in their approaches to objects and situations." Bernstein (1970) also comments on the fact that in carrying on a role-play type of conversation of the "he said/she said" variety, the child from the slum area is often richer and less hesitant in his speech, as if the more direct and concrete affective tone of human interaction were the preferred mode. Perhaps the "something else" is more thematic, personal, and concrete.

Let me then suggest a tentative conclusion from the first part of this much too condensed survey of class differences in language use. Bruner, Goodnow, and Austin (1956) drew a distinction between affective, functional, and formal categories. Affective categories involved the organization of events in terms of the immediate reactions they produced in the beholder, particular affect-laden reactions. Functional categories group objects and events in terms of fitness for the achievement of some particular goal or the carrying out of a particular task. Formal categories are those governed by a set of relatively universal criterial attributes in terms of which things can be placed without reference either to their use or to the "gut reaction" they produce.

It would seem to be the case, though I am aware of how very insufficient the data still are, that "middle-class upbringing" has the tendency to push the child toward a habitual use of formal categories and strategies appropriate to such categorizing—featural analysis of tasks, consideration of alternative possibilities, questioning and hypothesizing, and elaborating. It is a mode in which one uses language in a characteristic way: by constructing linguistically an analytic replica independent of the situation and its functional demands and manipulating the replica by the rules of language.

But note that it is *not* that children of different classes differ either in the *amount* of language that they "have," nor in the varient *rules* that govern their language. Cazden (1970) and Labov (1969) have compiled enough evidence from the extant literature to cast serious doubt on both the "less language" and the "different language" theories of class difference. The critical issue seems to be language *use* in a variety of *situations* and the manner in which home and subculture affects such usage. Or as Hymes (on press) puts it, children not only learn to form and interpret sentences but "also acquire knowledge of a set of ways in which sentences are used." A striking experiment by Heider, Cazden, and Brown (1968), and an observation by Francis Palmer (1968), remind us again that the lower-class child, under appropriate conditions, *can* operate analytically quite well, though he might ordinarily or habitually not do so. Heider, et al. asked lower-class and middle-class ten-year-old boys to describe a picture of an animal in a fashion that would later permit distinguishing it from many other similar pictures. Some of the attributes they used in their descriptions were criterial in the sense of uniquely defining the target or reducing materially the range of possibilities; others were irrelevant for guiding one to the correct target. Both groups mentioned about the same total number of attributes, and moreover, both mentioned about the same number of criterial attributes, 18 out of a total of 67 for middle-class boys, 16 out of 69 for lower-class. Where they differed was in the number of adult prompts and requests that were necessary to get the attributes out of them: an average of 6.11 for the lower-class children, and only 3.56 for the middle-class. And by the same token, Palmer (1968) finds that if seven or eight hours of prior, rapport-establishing contact is assured before testing, most differences between lower-class and middle-class children become minimal. This point was also established by Labov (1968) when he concluded that Northern Negro English did not differ structurally or in underlying logic from Standard English.

What seems to be at issue again is the question of "personalness" and the egocentric axis. If the situation is personal, egocentrically organized, then the lower-class child can be just as complex as the middle-class one. But the lower-class child seems far less able to achieve "decentration," to analyze things in the world from a perspective other than his personal or local perspective. Perhaps this point will become more compelling when we examine a second feature of language that differentiates between social classes, to which we turn now.*

This second feature involves communicating through language in a fashion independent of the situation. Grace de Laguna (1927) says, "The evolution of language is characterized by a progressive freeing of speech from dependence on the perceived conditions under which it is uttered and heard, and from the behavior which accompanies it." She argues that the superior power of a written language inheres in this freedom from the contexts of action and perception, that all of its "semantic markers," to use a more familiar contemporary term (Katz and Fodor, 1964), are inherent in the utterance

---

* For a fuller discussion of the uses of language in different cultures and subcultures, see Cole and Bruner (1971).

itself: they are "intrasemantic" rather than "extrasemantic."

Greenfield (1969) remarks on how the speech of techno-
logically oriented societies (in contrast to preliterate, more
traditionally oriented ones) becomes more like a written language in its increasing context-independence. The title of her
paper, "On Speaking a Written Language," is apposite not
only, I think, to the trend in spoken language from a preliterate
to a literate society, but also from working class to middle
class society in Western culture. Basil Bernstein (1970) provides an interesting reason for the class difference. "We can
see that the class system has affected the distribution of knowledge. Historically and now, only a tiny proportion of the
population has been socialized into knowledge at the level of
the metalanguages of control and innovation, whereas the
mass of population has been socialized into knowledge at the
level of context-tied operations . . . This suggests that we
might be able to distinguish between two orders of meaning.
One we would call universalistic, the other particularistic.
Universalistic meanings are those in which principles and
operations are made linguistically explicit, whereas particularistic orders of meaning are meanings in which principles and
operations are relatively linguistically implicit. If orders of
meaning are universalistic, then meanings are less tied to a
given context. The metalanguages of public forms of thought as
these apply to objects and persons realize meanings of a universalistic type. Where meanings have this characteristic, then
individuals have access to the grounds of their experience and
can change the grounds . . . Where the meaning system is
particularistic, much of the meaning is imbedded in the context
of the social relationship. In this sense the meanings are tied
to a context and may be restricted to those who share a similar
contextual history. Where meanings are universalistic, they are
in principle available to all, because the principles and operations have been made explicit and so public. I shall argue
that forms of socialization orient the child toward speech codes
which control access to relatively context-tied or relatively
context-independent meanings." In short, it is the parochializing
effect of a culture of poverty that keeps language tied to context, tied to common experience, and restricted to the habitual

ways of one's own group.

The comparative context dependence of the language of disadvantaged children shows up early. In Joan Tough's work (1970) on three- to four-year-olds from middle- and lower-class backgrounds in an English industrial city, the children were matched on Stanford-Binet scores and, roughly, on verbal output. "All of the children's 'items of representation' . . . were rated as to whether they required the presence of the concrete situation for effective communication. This concrete component constitutes 20.9 per cent of the representation of the favored children and 34.5 per cent of the less favored children. The most frequent form of the concrete component are pronouns whose only reference is to something pointed at in the environment. Such 'exophoric' reference is contrasted with 'anaphoric' reference, where pronouns refer to an antecedent previously supplied in words. The percentage of anaphoric references was 22.8 per cent for the favored children and only 7.7 per cent for the less favored. This finding replicated Bernstein's research with children five to seven years old (Hawkins, 1968)." I do not know, save by everyday observation, whether the difference is greater still among adults, but my impression is that the difference in decontextualization is greater between an English barrister and a dock worker than it is between their children.

Two trends, then, seem to be operative in the *use* of language by middle-class children. One is the use of language as an instrument of analysis-and-synthesis in problem solving, wherein the analytic power of language aids in abstraction or feature extraction, and the generative, transformational powers of language are used in reorganizing and synthesizing the features thus abstracted. The second trend is toward decontextualization, toward learning to use language without dependence upon shared percepts or actions, with sole reliance on the linguistic self-sufficiency of the message. Decontextualization permits information to be conceived as independent of the speaker's vantage point, it permits communications with those who do not share one's daily experience or actions, and in fact does, as Bernstein (1970) insists, allow one to transcend restrictions of locale and affiliation. Lower-class language, in contrast, is more affective and metaphoric than formal or analytic in its use, more given to narrative than to causal or generic form. It is more tied to place and affiliation, serving the interests of concrete familiarity rather than generality, more tied to finding than to seeking.

Both trends seem to reflect the kind of goal striving and problem solving characteristic of those who without protest have accepted occupancy of the bottom roles and statuses in the society that roughly constitute the position of poverty. It is not that the poor are "victims" of the system—they are, but so is everybody else in some way. It is rather that a set of values, a way of goal seeking, a way of dealing with means and ends become associated with poverty.

SOCIAL RECIPROCITY

Being socio-economically disadvantaged is no simple matter of deficit, of suffering a cultural avitaminosis that can be dosed by suitable inputs of compensation. It is a complex of circumstances at the center of which is usually a family whose wage earner is without a job or where there is no male wage earner. If there is a job, usually it is as demanding in status as it is unremunerative. The setting is a neighborhood that has adapted itself often with much human bravura to "being at the bottom," with little by way of long range perspective or hope, often alienated by a sense of ethnic separation from the main culture.

This is not the place to examine the economic, social, and political means whereby some societies segregate social classes by restricting access to knowledge and eroding in childhood the skills needed to gain and use knowledge. Obviously, the techniques of segregation by class are not deliberately planned, and they often resist deliberate efforts of abolition. More to the point is to ask how the behavior patterns of the dispossessed are transmitted by the family to produce the forms of coping associated with poverty (or middle-class status).

We have already encountered a striking difference in the use of reward and punishment by the mother. One finding suggests that the transmission may be accomplished by so simple a factor as rewarding achievement in the middle-class while punishing or ridiculing failure among children of the poor (Bee, et al., 1967). Several studies point to a by-product in the form of a class difference in asking adults for help (for example, Kohlberg, 1963) or in showing doubt in their presence (for example, Hawkins, 1968). The poor do much less of both.

Modeling of "class" patterns by adults—both in interaction with the child and in general—may be another source of family transmission. Hamburg (1968) draws some interesting inferences about such modeling from studies of higher primates. He writes, "The newer field studies suggest the adaptive significance of observational learning in a social context. Time and again, one observes the following sequence: (1) close observation of one animal by another; (2) imitation by the observing animal of the behavior of some observed animal; and (3) the later practice of the observed behavior, particularly in the play group of young animals." A like point is made for preliterate people, as in the close study of Talensee education and play by Fortes (1938) and the detailed observation of children's play among the Bushmen by Lorna Marshall (1963). They too point to the conclusion that observation and imitative incorporation in play is widespread and seemingly central.

Early language acquisition seems almost to be the type case of modeling. In a recent and detailed review of the language acquisition of the three children being studied at Harvard by Brown, Cazden, and Bellugi (1969), the importance of modeling is highlighted. But this work suggests that modeling is not a simple form of transmission.

The puzzling and challenging thing about learning language from a model is that the child is not so much copying specific language behavior from observation-and-imitation, but rather is developing general rules about how to behave from which various specific acts can be appropriately derived or interpreted. It is not at all clear how much we should attribute in early learning to the reinforcing effects of reward and/or punishment and how much to such rule learning acquired by observing or interacting with a model. Discussing the role of approval and disapproval as possible influences in the acquisition of grammar, Brown and his colleagues (1969) found, "In general, the parents fitted propositions to the child's utterances, however incomplete or distorted the utterances, and then approved or not according to the correspondence between proposition and reality. Thus *Her curl my hair* was approved because the mother was in fact curling Eve's hair. However, Sarah's grammatically impeccable, *There's the animal farmhouse* was disapproved because the building was a lighthouse. . . . It seems then to be truth value rather than syntactic well formedness that chiefly governs explicit verbal reinforcement by parents—which renders mildly paradoxical the fact that the usual product of such a training schedule is an adult whose speech is highly grammatical but not notably truthful."

If it turns out to be the case that the young child is learning not only linguistic rules but also "rules about roles" and rules also about *ways* of thinking and *ways* of talking, then indoctrination in class patterns must be, in the linguist's sense, generative and pervasive to a degree that is difficult to estimate. This would make even more meaningful the insistence of Smilansky (1968) that intervention programs emphasize *rationale* and *explanation* in order to reach the deep conceptual level where the class-pattern rules operate. In sum, both through the compelling effects of approval and disapproval and by the modeling of "rule-bound" behavior, the family passes on class patterns of goal striving, problem solving, paying attention, and so forth.

Let me, in closing this section, make one thing clear. I am *not* arguing that middle-class culture is good for all or even good for the middle-class. Indeed, its denial of the problem of dispossession, poverty, and privilege make it contemptible in the eyes of even compassionate critics. Nor do I argue that the culture of the dispossessed is not rich and varied within its limits. (There are critics, like Baratz and Baratz [1970], who are too ready to cry "racist" to what they sense to be derogation of Black culture, or Yemeni culture, or Cockney culture.) But, in effect, insofar as a subculture represents a reaction to defeat and insofar as it is caught by a sense of powerlessness, it suppresses the potential of those who grow up under its sway by discouraging problem solving. The source of powerlessness that such a subculture generates, no matter how moving its byproducts, produces instability in the society and unfulfilled promise in human beings (Cole and Bruner, 1971).

CULTURE AND THEORIES OF DEVELOPMENT

Thus far we have concentrated upon how a culture of poverty reflects itself in child rearing. But there is no reason to believe that the effects of such child rearing are either inevitable or irreversible—there are ways of altering the impact of middle-class pressures or of poverty. Better to appreciate this likelihood of change, we must look briefly at the nature of human development and at theories designed to explicate it.

There is a paradox in contemporary formulations. We have, on the one hand, rejected the idea of culture-free intelligence, and probably the Coleman Report (1966) put the finishing blow to the idea of school-free tests of intelligence. In this view, intelligence depends on the incorporation of culture. At the same time, there is a current vogue for theories of intellectual development promoting education strategies that presumably are unaffected (or virtually unaffected) by class difference, cultural background, and other conditions of the life of the child, short, perhaps, of pathology. The only differences, according to such theories, are in time table, the steps being the same. It is a matter only of slower and faster, not of difference in kind. So on the one side we urge a context-sensitive view while on the other we propose that intelligence grows from the inside out with support from the environment being only in the form of aliments appropriate to the stage of development—a relatively context-free conception formulated most comprehensively by Piaget's Geneva School.

I suspect both kinds of theory are necessary—at least they have always existed. The strength of a context-free view is that it searches for universal structures of mind; its weakness is its intrinsic anticulturalism. Aebli (1970) notes the Geneva dilemma: if the child only takes in what he is "ready to assimilate," why bother to teach before he is ready, and since he takes it in naturally once he *is* ready, why bother afterwards? The weakness of most context-sensitive views of development is that they give too much importance to individual and cultural differences and overlook the universals of growth. Their strength, of course, is in a sensitivity to the nature of the human plight and how this plight is fashioned by culture.

Two things, it seems to me, can keep us mindful of both universality and cultural diversity. The first is an appreciation of the universals of human culture, which revolve most often around reciprocal exchange through symbolic, affiliative, and economic systems. To alter man's participation in any of these systems of exchange is to force a change in how man carries out the enterprises of life. For what must be adjusted to is precisely these exchange systems—what we come to expect by way of respect, affiliation, and goods. Herein is where poverty is so crucial an issue—for poverty in economic life affects family structure, affects one's symbolic sense of worth, one's feeling of control. But beyond the universals of culture, there are universals in man's primate heritage. The primate series illustrates to an extraordinary degree the emergence of curiosity, play, planfulness, anticipation, and, ultimately, the ways of seeking, transforming, representing, and using information that characterize the human species. This review thus far has surely shown us how hope, confidence, and a sense of the future can affect the unfolding and nurturing of these capacities. If the conditions imposed by a culture can alter hopes and shrink confidence, it can surely alter the use of these species-typical patterns of behavior. Theories of development are guides for understanding the perfectibility of man as well as his vulnerability. They define man's place in nature and signal opportunities for improving or changing his lot by aiding growth. A theory of development that specifies nothing about intervention is blind to culture. One that specifies only intervention is blind to man's biological inheritance.

ON INTERVENTION

With respect to virtually any criterion of equal opportunity and equal access to opportunity, the children of the poor, and particularly the urban poor, are plainly not getting as much schooling, or getting as much from their schooling, as their middle-class age mates. By any conservative estimate of what happens before school, about a half million of the roughly four million children of each year of age in the United States are receiving substandard fare in day-care, nursery school, kindergarten, guidance, whatnot. This is not intended as a psychological assessment but as a description of resources, of officially agreed-upon facilities (see Sugarman, 1970). A few typical figures make the matter of facilities concrete. The kindergarten population in the United States in 1966 was 3,000,000 out of approximately 12,000,000 of the age group three through five. And the chances of a child in the lowest quarter of income being in kindergarten were immeasurably less than those of a child in the top quarter. In 1967, there were 193,000 children in full-year Headstart, a definite improvement but a fraction of the estimated 20 per cent of the 8,000,000 three- and four-year-olds who needed it, or 1,600,000. One should note that more than 80 per cent of parents covered in the Westinghouse study (1969) said that their children improved as a result of Headstart, a fact to be reckoned with in the light of the Rosenthal effect (1968) and Graves's (1969) findings on the ebbing confidence of poor urban mothers in their children. Finally, in 1968 there were some 2.2 million working mothers in America, many the sole breadwinner in the family, with children three to five years of age. In that same year, there were approximately 310,000 places for children in registered day-care centers and in approved "private home" arrangements, one place per seven mothers. The present estimate, as of 1970, is that 9 per cent of children two to five or 14 per cent of children three to five with working mothers are cared for in day-care centers.

I have been expressing the view that induction into this "culture of failure" begins early. In cities like New York, half the children born in poverty are illegitimate. Growing up in an urban ghetto, in the family structure often produced by such a setting, in the neighborhoods and schools that it spawns, surely diminishes the skills and confidence needed to use the benefits of modern industrial, democratic society on one's own behalf or on behalf of one's own group. Romanticism about poverty and its effects on growth is middle-class escapism.

Probably we cannot change this plight without changing the society that permitted such poverty to exist during a time of affluence. My first recommendation as a common-sense psychologist and as a concerned man is to transform radically the structure of our society. But that is not our topic. What can one do now, within the context of the changing society of today?

At a symposium on the "Education of the Infant and Young Child" at the American Association for the Advancement of Science late in 1969 (Denenberg, 1970), I was asked to prepare a summary of reports on major programs of intervention. Several themes common to the reports struck me.

The first was that there is an enormous influence exerted by the child's day-to-day caretaker, whatever the program. And programs had to consider the mother as a major factor. She had to be worked with, not compensated for.

Second, growth involves a small, step-wise acquisition of skill and competence on a day-to-day basis. Though theories of development emphasize principally the great leaps forward, it is in the management of day-to-day progress that discouragement or encouragement occur, where shaping has effect toward progress in one direction or another.

Third, there is an enormous contribution to cognitive development from factors that, on the surface, are anything but traditionally cognitive. They are, instead, diffuse affective factors: confidence, the capacity to control one's environment, hope in the future, and the like. They too operate day-to-day, and they reflect the caretaker's mood.

Fourth, it is now widely agreed that the idea of "enrichment" puts the child in the position of a passive consumer. One study after another showed that for a child to benefit he must be helped to be on his own, to operate eventually on his own activation. It is this activation that must be cultivated and supported.

Fifth, and very practically, there seems to be a wide range of alternative ways to succeed in an intervention program, the provision for success being that they produce opportunities for mother and child to carry out activities that have some structure to them.

Beyond these specific conclusions, a general one stood out: the importance of initiative in the community as a means of activating parents and caretakers to do something for their children.

Haggstrom (1964) again makes telling points in discussing "the power of the poor."

> In order to reduce poverty-related psychological and social problems in the United States, the major community will have to change its relationship to neighborhoods of poverty in such a fashion that families in the neighborhoods have a greater stake in the broader society and can more successfully participate in the decision making process . . . The poor must as a group be helped to secure opportunities for themselves. Only then will motivation be released that is now locked in the silent and usually successful battle of the neighborhoods of poverty to maintain themselves in an alien social world. This motivation . . . will enable them to enter the majority society and make it as nurturant of them as it is at present of the more prosperous . . . One way in which the poor can remedy the psychological consequences of their powerlessness and of the image of the poor as worthless is for them to undertake social action that redefines them . . . To be effective such social action should have the following characteristics:
> 1. The poor see themselves as the source of action.
> 2. The action affects in major ways the preconceptions, values, or interests of [those] defining the poor.
> 3. The action demands much in effort and skill.
> 4. The action ends in success.
> 5. The successful self-originated important action is seen to increase the symbolic value of specific people who are poor.

Haggstrom's list is admittedly ambitious. Even so, it falls short of dealing with some intractable correlates of poverty, as race in the case of the American Black, as nationality with the Italian Swiss, and so on. Yet it surely provides a sense of the role of community action in providing a background for countering the very problems of goal seeking, problem solving, and language usage we have been discussing.

Granted the importance of community action and revolutionary aspirations in the struggle against poverty's effects, one can still discuss psychological help for the child of poverty so that he may grow more effectively, not into a middle-class suburban child (who has problems of his own) but into one capable of helping himself and his own community more effectively. It is with some considerations along these lines that I should like to conclude.

The expression "no room at the bottom" means something. With an increase in technological complexity, capital-intensive rather than labor-intensive techniques come to prevail. Instead of *more* labor to run the economy, more intensively *skilled* labor is used. While school rejects can be absorbed in a society built on stoop-labor, they can no longer find a place in one where even the street sweeper gives way to well designed, motorized brushing machines. Since the first steps toward dropping out take place at home, the home is where the first remedies must be applied—only the first, for it avails little to give help in the nursery only to defeat the child later in school.

The objective of "curricula" for young children (as for older ones) is to produce the kind of generalist in skill, the "skill intensive" worker who is capable of acting as a controlling factor in the regulating, running, or curbing of a technology such as we are developing in the West, or one who is capable of understanding it well enough to serve, to criticize, to be controller rather than victim. I am assuming, to put it plainly, that man's cultural and biological evolution is toward general skill and intelligence and that the major difficulty we face is not in achieving such skill but in devising a society that can use it wisely. This means a society in which man feels at home and fulfilled enough to strive and to use his gifts. I am taking for granted that we do *not* want to curb idiosyncrasy, surprise, and the inevitable raucousness that goes with freedom.

My colleagues at the Center for Cognitive Studies, Drs. Greenfield and Tronick, have been devising a curriculum for a day-care center at Bromley Heath in the Roxbury section of Boston. I have been enormously impressed with a set of implicit principles underlying their work (hopefully soon to be published)—principles that I have extracted from one of their memoranda, but with which they may not agree. Nonetheless, let me briefly run through them, with a view not toward comprehensiveness but toward illustration. These will be many echoes from earlier parts of this paper.

1. *The active organism.* Human intelligence is active and seeking. It needs an environment to encourage such action.
2. *Effort after meaning.* The search for meaning and regularity begins at birth. There is a constant search for cues for significance that need nurturing.
3. *Intentionality.* Action and the search for meaning are guided by intention, self-directed, and help can be provided to sustain such self-direction.
4. *Pace.* Each age and activity has a pace that requires respect and patience from those around the baby.
5. *Receptivity and state.* There is a state of alert, awake receptivity when the child is hospitable to the environment. Use it for getting to the infant, rather than trying to break through unreceptive states.
6. *Cycles of competence.* Each newly emerging skill has a cycle of competence: initial crude effort, followed by consolidation and perfecting, followed by a period of variation. These phases require recognition to be helped to their completion.
7. *Prerequisites.* Skills require prior skills for mastery, as, for example, in the infant's "fail-safe" method of sitting down from a standing position before he risks walking. Opportunity to master prerequisites helps later skills.
8. *Appropriateness of play and objects.* Different activities have requirements that can be met by providing appropriate games, play, or objects. The child intent on exploring small irregularities with his fingers will work for hours on a board with irregular holes cut in it, each differently colored.
9. *Principles of the enterprise.* Activity, as the child grows older is more temporally organized under the control of intention. It is dependent upon mobilizing means to achieve an objective. Provision of means and encouragement for such enterprises and protection from distraction is of utmost importance to growth.
10. *Principle of representation.* Useful memory depends upon finding effective ways of representing information—be it

in customary action, in a well-liked game, in a vivid picture, or in words. Marking something for later use or recognition is an important aspect of growth.

11. *Analysis and synthesis.* Problem solving often consists of reducing a task or situation to its component parts and then reorganizing them. Taking apart and putting together games, objects, stories, and problems is practice for such activity.

12. *Time perspective.* Each human being constructs the future by coming to expect, by planning and achieving planned objectives, by doing one thing so one may do the next, by learning how to hope and anticipate with realistic confidence. The process is long and begins early—probably with peek-a-boo.

13. *Principle of attachment.* Human young more than any other, perhaps, are dependent on a consistent caretaker who is there with warmth, certainty and effectiveness. It is in interaction with a caretaker that much of earliest learning occurs. A well-informed, decently satisfied, and hopeful caretaker is worth a pound of cure.

SUMMARY AND CONCLUSION

Persistent poverty over generations creates a culture of survival. Goals are short range, restricted. The outsider and the outside are suspect. One stays inside and gets what one can. Beating the system takes the place of using the system.

Such a culture of poverty gets to the young early—in how they learn to set goals, mobilize means, delay or fail to delay gratification. Very early too they learn in-group talk and thinking, and just as their language use reflects less long-range goal analysis, it tends toward a parochialism that makes it increasingly difficult to move or work outside the poverty neighborhood and the group. Make no mistake about it: it is a rich culture, intensely personalized and full of immediate rather than remote concerns. The issue is certainly not cultural deprivation, to be handled, like avitaminosis, with a massive dose of compensatory enrichment.

Rather the issue is to make it possible for the poor to gain a sense of their own power—through jobs, through community activation, through creating a sense of project in the future. Jobs, community action under community control, a decent revision of preschool and early school opportunities, all of these are crucial. But just as crucial is a sense of the change in the times, the insistence of the powerless that their plight is *not* a visitation of fate but a remediable condition. If we cannot produce that kind of change, then our system that has worked fairly well (if exploitatively) since the industrial revolution will doubtless collapse, probably to be replaced by something premised far more on coercion for all rather than just for some. That is why the generation to be raised is so crucial a resource. It may be our last chance.

REFERENCES CITED

AEBLI, H. Paper presented at the Center for Cognitive Studies, Harvard University, June 5, 1970.

AGASSIZ, J. Can religion go beyond reason? *Zygon, Journal of Religion and Science,* June 1969, *IV*(2).

ALLPORT, F. H. *Theories of perception and the concept of structure.* New York: Wiley, 1961.

ALLPORT, G. W. Effect: A secondary principle of learning. *Psychological Review,* 1946, *53,* 335–347.

ALLPORT, G. W., & PETTIGREW, T. F. Cultural influence on the perception of movement: The trapezoidal illusion among Zulus. *Journal of Abnormal and Social Psychology,* 1957, *55,* 104–113.

BARATZ, S. S., & BARATZ, J. C. Early childhood intervention: The social science base of institutional racism. *Harvard Educational Review,* Feb. 1970, *40*(1).

BARKER, R. On the nature of the environment. *Journal of Social Issues,* 1963, *19,* 17–38.

BARTLETT, F. C. *Remembering.* Cambridge, England: Cambridge Univer. Press, 1932.

BAYLEY, NANCY, & SCHAEFFER, E. S. Correlations of maternal and child behaviors with the development of mental abilities: Data from the Berkeley Growth Study. *Monographs of the Society for Research in Child Development,* 1964, *29*(6).

BEE, HELEN L., *et al.* Social class differences in maternal teaching strategies and speech patterns. *Developmental Psychology,* 1969, *1*(6), 726–734.

BERNSTEIN, B. Social class, language, and socialization. Unpublished paper, 1970.

BERNSTEIN, B. Social class and linguistic development: A theory of social learning. In A. H. Halsey, J. Floyd, & C. A. Anderson (Eds.), *Education, economy, and society.* New York: Free Press, 1961.

BERNSTEIN, N. *The coordination and regulation of movements.* Oxford: Pergamon, 1967.

BIESHEUVEL, S. *African intelligence.* Johannesburg: South African Institute of Race Relations, 1943.

BIESHEUVEL, S. Aspects of Africa. *The Listener,* 1956, *55,* 447–449.

BIESHEUVEL, S. *The human resources of the Republic of South Africa and their development.* Johannesburg: Witwatersrand Univer. Press, 1963.

BIESHEUVEL, S. Psychological tests and their application to non-European peoples. In *The Yearbook of Education.* London: Evans, 1949. Pp. 87–126.

BLANK, MARION, & SOLOMON, FRANCES. A tutorial language program to develop abstract thinking in socially disadvantaged preschool children. *Child Development,* 1968, 39, 379–389.

BLANK, MARION, & SOLOMON, FRANCES. How shall the disadvantaged child be taught? *Child Development,* March 1969, *40*(1), 47–61.

BLOOM, B. S. *Stability and change in human characteristics.* New York: Wiley, 1964.

BLOOM, B., & BRODER, L. Problem solving processes of college students. *Supplementary Educational Monograph, No. 73.* Chicago: Univer. Chicago Press, 1950.

BOAS, F. *The mind of primitive man.* New York: Macmillan, 1938.

BOGORAS, W. G. *The Chukchee.* New York: G. E. Stechert, 1904–1909. Part 1, *Material culture,* 1904; Part 3, *Social organization,* 1909.

BONTE, M. The reaction of two African societies to the Müller-Lyer illusion, *Journal of Social Psychology,* 1962, *58,* 265–268.

BROWN, R. *Words and things.* Glencoe: Free Press, 1958.

BROWN, R., CAZDEN, C. G., & BELLUGI, U. The child's grammar from I to III. In J. P. Hill (Ed.), *1967 Minnesota Symposium on Child Psychology.* Minneapolis: Univer. Minnesota Press, 1969. Pp. 28–73.

BROWN, R. & LENNEBERG, E. H. A study in language and cognition. *Journal of Abnormal and Social Psychology,* 1954, *49,* 454–462. Reprinted in S.

Saporta (Ed.), *Psycholinguistics: A book of readings.* New York: Holt, 1961. Pp. 480–492.

BRUNER, J. S. The course of cognitive growth. *American Psychologist,* 1964, *19,* 1–15.

BRUNER, J. S. Man: A course of study. *Educational Services Inc. Quarterly Report,* Spring-Summer, 1965, 3–13.

BRUNER, J. S., On going beyond the information given. In H. Gruber, *et al.* (Eds.), *Contemporary approaches to cognition.* Cambridge: Harvard Univer. Press, 1957.

BRUNER, J. S., Origins of problem solving strategies in skill acquisition. Presented at the XIX International Congress of Psychology, London, July 1969.

BRUNER, J. S., Personality dynamics and the process of perceiving. In R. R. Blake & G. V. Ramsey (Eds.), *Perception: an approach to personality.* New York: Ronald Press, 1951.

BRUNER, J. S., GOODNOW, JACQUELINE, & AUSTIN, G. A. *A study of thinking.* New York: Wiley, 1956.

BRUNER, J. S., LYONS, K., & KAYE, K. The growth of human manual intelligence. In preparation.

BRUNER, J. S. OLVER, ROSE R., GREENFIELD, PATRICIA M., *et al. Studies in cognitive growth.* New York: Wiley, 1966.

BRUNER, J. S., POSTMAN, L., & RODRIGUES, J. Expectation and the perception of color. *American Journal of Psychology,* 1951, *64,* 216–227.

BUTLER, R. A. Incentive conditions which influence visual exploration. *Journal of Experimental Psychology,* 1954, *48,* 19–23.

CARROLL, J. B., & CASAGRANDE, J. B. The function of language classifications in behavior. In Eleanor Maccoby, T. M. Newcomb & E. L. Hartley (Eds.), *Readings in social psychology.* New York: Holt, 1958. Pp. 18–31.

CAZDEN, C. B. Language education: learning that, learning how, learning to. Paper presented at meeting of the Boston Colloquium for the Philosophy of Education, Boston University, April 13, 1970.

CAZDEN, C. B. The neglected situation: a source of social class differences in language use. *Journal of Social Issues,* 1970, *3.*

CAZDEN, C. B. The neglected situation in child language research and education. In F. Williams (Ed.), *Language and poverty: Perspectives on a theme.* Chicago: Markham, 1970. Pp. 81–101.

CLARK, W. E. L. *The antecedents of man.* Edinburgh: Edinburgh Univer. Press, 1959.

CLARK, W. E. L. *Man-apes or ape-men?: The story of discoveries in Africa.* New York: Holt, 1967.

COLE, M., & BRUNER, J. S. Some preliminaries to a theory of cultural differences. *Psychological Review,* in press.

COLEMAN, J. S., *et al. Equality of Educational Opportunity.* Washington, D.C.: U. S. Dept. of Health, Education, and Welfare, Office of Education, 1966

COVINGTON, M. V., CRUTCHFIELD, R. S., & DAVIES, L. B. *The productive thinking program.* Berkeley: Educational Innovation, 1966. (Augmented edition, in press, Columbus, Ohio: Merrill.)

CRYNS, A. G. J. African intelligence: A critical survey of cross-cultural intelligence research in Africa south of the Sahara. *Journal of Social Psychology,* 1964, *57,* 283–301.

DART, R. The bone tool-manufacturing ability of *Australopithecus prometheus. American Anthropology,* 1960, *62,* 134–143.

DENENBERG, V. H. (Ed.). Proceedings of the American Association for the Advancement of Science Symposium on *Education of the Infant and Young Child.* (Boston, December 1969). New York: Academic Press, 1970.

DEUTSCH, M. The role of social class in language development and cognition. *American Journal of Orthopsychiatry,* 1965, *35,* 78–88.

DOOB, L. W. The effect of codability upon the afferent and efferent functioning of language. *Journal of Social Psychology,* 1960, *52,* 3–15.

DOUVAN, ELIZABETH. Social status and success striving. *Journal of Abnormal and Social Psychology*, 1956, *52*, 219–223.

DURKHEIM, E., & MAUSS, M. *Primitive classification*. Chicago: Univer. Chicago Press, 1963.

EBBINGHAUS, H. *Memory: A contribution to experimental psychology*. New York: Teachers College, Columbia University, 1913.

FESTINGER, L. *A theory of cognitive dissonance*. Stanford: Stanford Univer. Press, 1962.

FLAVELL, J. *The developmental psychology of Jean Piaget*. Princeton: Van Nostrand, 1963.

FORTES, M. Social and psychological aspects of education in Taleland. Supplement to *Africa*, 1938, *11*(4).

FROEBEL, F. W. *Autobiography*. Syracuse, New York: C. W. Bardeen, 1890. Selections reprinted in *Three thousand years of educational wisdom*, ed. R. Ulich, Cambridge, Mass.: Harvard Univer. Press, 1947.

GAY, J. H. Education and mathematics among the Kpelle of Liberia. Paper read at Commission Interunions de l'Enseignement des Sciences, Dakar, Jan. 1965.

GAY, J. H., & COLE, M. *The new mathematics and an old culture: A study of learning among the Kpelle*. New York: Holt, 1967.

Goals for school mathematics. Cambridge Conference on School Mathematics. Boston: Houghton, 1963.

GOODALL, JANE: Chimpanzees of the Gombe Stream Reserve. In I. DeVore (Ed.), *Primate behavior: Field studies of monkeys and apes*. New York: Holt, 1965.

GOODNOW, JACQUELINE, & PETTIGREW, T. Effect of prior patterns of experience on strategies and learning sets. *Journal of Experimental Psychology*, 1955, *49*, 381–389.

GRAVES, NANCY B. City, country, and childrearing in three cultures. Institute of Behavioral Sciences, University of Colorado, 1969.

GREENFIELD, PATRICIA M. Oral or written language: The consequence for cognitive development in Africa and the United States. Symposium on Cross-Cultural Cognitive Studies, American Educational Research Association, Chicago, Feb. 9, 1968.

GREENFIELD, PATRICIA M. Goal as environmental variable in the development of intelligence. Presented at Conference on Contributions to Intelligence, University of Illinois, Urbana, Nov. 15, 1969.

GREGORY, R. L. *Eye and brain*. New York: McGraw-Hill, 1966.

HAGGSTROM, W. The power of the poor. In F. Fiessman, J. Cohen, & A. Pearl (Eds.), *Mental health of the poor*. New York: Free Press, 1964.

HAMBURG, D. Evolution of emotional responses: Evidence from recent research on nonhuman primates. *Science and Psychoanalysis, XII*, 1968.

HARLOW, H. F. Mice, monkeys, men, and motives. *Psychological Review*, 1953, *60*, 23–32.

HAWKINS, P. R. Social class, the nominal group, and reference. Sociological Research Unit, University of London, Institute of Education, 1968.

HEIDER, E. R., CAZDEN, C. B., & BROWN, R. Social class differences in the effectiveness and style of children's coding ability. *Project Literacy Reports, No. 9*, Ithaca: Cornell Univer. Press, 1968. Pp. 1–10.

HEIDER, F. *The psychology of interpersonal relations*. New York: Wiley, 1958.

HELD, R., & HEIN, A. V. Adaptation of disarranged hand-eye coordination contingent upon reafferent stimulation. *Perceptual and Motor Skills*, 1958, *8*, 87–90.

HESS, R. D., & SHIPMAN, VIRGINIA C. Early experience and socialization of cognitive modes in children. *Child Development*, 1965, *36*, 869–886.

HESS, R. D., & SHIPMAN, VIRGINIA C. Maternal influences upon early learning: The cognitive environments of urban preschool children. In R. D. Hess & R. M. Bear (Eds.), *Early Education*, Chicago: Aldine, 1968.

HESS, R. D., et al. *The cognitive environments of urban preschool children*. The Graduate School of Education, University of Chicago, 1969.

VON HOLST, E., & MITTLESTAEDT, H. Das reafferenzprinzip. *Naturwissenschaften*, 1950, *37*, 464–476.

HORNER, V. M. The verbal world of the lower-class three year old: A pilot study in linguistic ecology. Unpublished doctoral dissertation, University of Rochester, 1968.

HUDSON, W. Pictorial depth perception in subcultural groups in Africa. *Journal of Social Psychology*, 1960, *52*, 183–208.

HYMES, D. On communication competence. In R. Huxley & E. Ingram (Eds.), *The Mechanism of language development*. London: Ciba Foundation, in press.

The impact of Head Start: An evaluation of the effects of Head Start experience on children's cognitive and affective development. Westinghouse Learning Corporation, Ohio University, March 1969.

INHELDER, B., & PIAGET, J. *Growth of logical thinking from childhood to adolescence*. New York: Basic Books, 1958.

ITANI, J. On the acquisition and propagation of a new food habit in the natural group of the Japanese monkey at Takasakiyama. *Primates*, 1958, *1*(2), 84–98. (In Japanese.)

JAHODA, J. Assessment of abstract behavior in a non-Western culture. *Journal of Abnormal and Social Psychology*, 1956, *53*, 237–243.

JOHANSEN, M. The experienced continuation of some three-dimensional forms. *Acta Psychologia*, 1957, *13*, 1–26.

KAGAN, J., & MOSS, H. A. *Birth to maturity: A study in psychological development*. New York: Wiley, 1962.

KALNINS, ILZE. The use of sucking in instrumental learning. Presented as doctoral thesis at the University of Toronto, 1970.

KARDINER, A. Lecture at Harvard University, Cambridge, Mass., April 1965.

KATZ, J. J., & FODOR, J. A. The structure of a semantic theory. In J. A. Fodor & J. J. Katz (Eds.), *The structure of language: Readings in the philosophy of language*. Englewood Cliffs: Prentice-Hall, 1964.

KAWAMURA, S. The process of sub-culture propagation among Japanese macaques. *Primates*, 1959 *2*(1), 43–60.

KESTELOOF, LILYAN. *Aimé Césaire*. Paris: Editions Press Seghers, 1962.

KLAUS, R., & GRAY, S. The early training project for disadvantaged children: A report after five years. *Monographs of the Society for Research in Child Development*, 1968, *33*(4).

KLUCKHOHN, C. *Mirror for man*. New York: Whittlesey House, 1949.

KLUCKHOHN, FLORENCE R., & STRODTBECK, F. L. *Variations in value orientations*. Evanston: Row, Peterson, 1961.

KOEN, F. The codability of complex stimuli: Three modes of representation. Unpublished paper, University of Michigan, Ann Arbor, 1965.

KOFFKA, K. *Principles of Gestalt psychology*. New York: Harcourt, Brace, 1935.

KOHLBERG, L. Summary of students' findings from behavioral observations they made in a psychology course given at the University of Chicago, 1963.

KÖHLER, W. *Dynamics in psychology*. New York: Liveright, 1940.

KÖHLER, W. Psychological remarks on some questions of anthropology. *American Journal of Psychology*, 1937, *58*, 271–288. Reprinted in Mary Henle (Ed.), *Documents of Gestalt psychology*. Berkeley: Univer. California Press, 1961. Pp. 203–221.

LABOV, W. The logic of non-standard English. In James Alatis (Ed.), *Georgetown Monograph Series on Language and Linguistics*, 1969, *22*.

DE LAGUNA, G. A. *Speech: Its function and development*. Bloomington: Indiana Univer. Press, 1927.

LANTZ, DELEE. Color naming and color recognition: A study in the psychology of language. Unpublished doctoral dissertation, Harvard University, 1963.

LANTZ, DELEE, & STEFFLRE, V. Language and cognition revisited. *Journal of Abnormal and Social Psychology*, 1964, *69*, 472–481.

LASHLEY, K. The problem of serial order in behavior. In L. A. Jeffress (Ed.),

Cerebral mechanisms in behavior: The Hixon symposium. New York: Wiley, 1951.

LAUGHLIN, W. Hunting: An integrating biobehavior system and its evolutionary importance. In I. DeVore & R. B. Lee (Eds.), *Man the hunter.* Chicago: Aldine, 1968. Pp. 304–320.

LEACH, E. We scientists have the right to play God. *Saturday Evening Post,* Nov. 1968, *23*, 16ff. (Reith Lectures, BBC, Fall 1968.)

LENNEBERG, E. H. Color naming, color recognition, color discrimination: A reappraisal. *Perceptual and Motor Skills,* 1961, *12*, 375–383.

LENNEBERG, E. H., & ROBERTS, J. M. The language of experience: A study in methodology. *International Journal of American Living, Supplement,* 1956, *22* (Memoir 13).

LEVI-STRAUSS, C. Anthropology: Its achievements and future. Lecture presented at Bicentennial Celebration, Smithsonian Institution, Washington, D.C., September 1965.

LEVI-STRAUSS, C. *La pensée sauvage.* Paris: Plon, 1962.

LEVI-STRAUSS, C. The structural study of myth. In *Structural anthropology.* (Trans. by Claire Jacobson & B. Grundfest Scharpf.) New York: Basic Books, 1963. Pp. 206–231.

LEWIS, O. *The children of Sanchez.* New York: Random House, 1961.

LEWIS, O. The culture of poverty. *Scientific American.* Oct. 1966, *215*(4). Pp. 19–25.

LINDZEY, G. *Projective techniques and cross-cultural research.* New York: Appleton, 1961.

LIPSITT, L. P. Learning in the human infant. In H. W. Stevenson, E. H. Hess, & Harriet L. Rheingold (Eds.), *Early behavior: Comparative and developmental approach.* New York: Wiley, 1967.

LOTT, A. J., & LOTT, BERNICE E. *Negro and white youth.* New York: Holt, 1963.

LURIA, A. R. *The role of speech in regulation of normal and abnormal behavior.* New York: Liveright, 1961.

McGRAW, MYRTLE B. *A study of Johnny and Jimmy.* New York: Appleton, 1935.

MACH, E. *The analysis of sensation.* Chicago: Open Court Publishing Co., 1914.

MACKWORTH, N. H., & BRUNER, J. S. How adults and children search and recognize pictures. *Human Development,* in press, 1970.

MACLAY, H. An experimental study of language and non-linguistic behavior. *Southwestern Journal of Anthropology,* 1958, *14*, 220–229.

McNEILL, D. Anthropological psycholinguistics. Unpublished paper, Harvard University, 1965.

MARSHALL, L., & MARSHALL, LORNA. The bushmen of Kalihari. *National Geographic,* 1963, 23(6). Pp. 866–888.

MEAD, MARGARET. Research on primitive children. In L. Carmichael (Ed.), *Manual of child psychology.* New York: Wiley, 1946. Pp. 735–789.

MEDAWAR, P. Onwards from Spencer: Evolution and evolutionism. *Encounter,* 1963, *21*, 35–43.

MILLER, G. A. Computers, communication, and cognition. *Advancement of Science,* January 1965, *21*, 417–430.

MILLER, G. A. The magical number 7, plus or minus 2: Some limits on our capacity for processing information. *Psychological Review,* 1956, *63*, 81–97.

MILLER, G. A., GALANTER, E., & PRIBRAM, K. H. *Plans and the structure of behavior.* New York: Holt, 1960.

MOFFETT, J. *Teaching the universe of discourse.* Boston: Houghton, 1968.

MONTEIL, V. *L'Islam noir.* Paris: Editions du Seuil, 1964.

MORRISON, P. Less may be more. *American Journal of Physics,* 1964, *32*, 441–457.

MUNDY-CASTLE, A. C., & ANGLIN, J. The development of looking in infancy. Presented at Biennial Conference of the Society for Research in Child Development, Santa Monica, California, April 1969.

MUSSEN, P. H., URBANO, P., & BOUTERLINE-YOUNG, H. Esplorazione dei motivi per mezzo di un reattivo: II. Classi sociali e motivazione fra adolescenti di origine italiana (Exploration of motives through a projective technique). *Arch. Psicol. Neurol. Psichiat.*, 1961, *22*, 681–690.

NEISSER, U. *Cognitive psychology.* New York: Appleton, 1967.

NEWELL, A., SHAW, J. D., & SIMON, H. A. Elements of a theory of human problem solving. *Psychological Review*, 1958, *65*, 151–166.

OAKLEY, K. P. *Man the tool maker* (4th Ed.). Chicago: Chicago Univer. Press, 1960.

OGDEN, C. K., & RICHARDS, I. A. *The meaning of meaning* (3rd Rev. Ed.). New York: Harcourt, Brace, 1930.

PALMER, F. Unpublished research reported at a colloquium at Harvard University, Nov. 1968. Cited in Kagan, J. S. Inadequate evidence and illogical conclusions, *Harvard Educational Review*, Spring 1969, *39*(2).

PAPOUSEK, H. Experimental studies of appetitional behavior in human newborns and infants. In H. W. Stevenson, E. H. Hess, & H. L. Rheingold, *Early behavior: Comparative and developmental approaches.* New York: Wiley, 1967.

PIAGET, J. *The child's conception of number.* New York: Humanities Press, 1952.

PIAGET, J. *The child's conception of physical causality.* London: Kegan Paul, 1930.

PIAGET, J. *The construction of reality in the child.* New York: Basic Books, 1954.

PIAGET, J. *The origins of intelligence in children.* New York: International Universities Press, 1952.

PRICE-WILLIAMS, D. R. A study concerning concepts of conservation of quantities among primitive children. *Acta Psychologica.* Amsterdam, 1961, *18*, 297–305.

RABAIN-ZEMPLÉNI, JACQUELINE. Quelques réfléxions sur les modes fondamentaux de relations chez l'enfant wolof du sevrage à l'intégration dans la classe d'âge. Paris: Association Universitaire pour le Développement de l'Enseignement et de la Culture en Afrique et à Madagascar, 1965.

RANKEN, H. B. Language and thinking: Positive and negative effects of naming. *Science*, 1963, *141*, 48–50.

RIVERS, W. H. R. Observations on the senses of the Todas. *British Journal of Psychology*, 1905, 322–396.

ROBINSON, H. B., & ROBINSON, N. M. The problem of timing in preschool education. In R. D. Hess & R. M. Bear (Eds.), *Early Education.* Chicago: Aldine, 1968.

ROBINSON, W. P., & CREED, C. D. Perceptual and verbal discriminations of "elaborated" and "restricted" code users. *Language and Speech*, 1968, *11*. Pp. 182–193.

ROSENTHAL, R., & JACOBSON, L. *Pygmalion in the classroom.* New York: Holt, 1968.

SAPIR, E. *Language: An introduction to the study of speech.* New York: Harcourt, Brace, 1921.

SCHAEFER, E. S. Need for early and continuing education. In V. H. Denenberg (Ed.), *Proceedings of the AAAS Symposium on Education of the Infant and Young Child* (Boston, Dec. 1969). London: Academic Press, in press.

SCHOGGEN, MAXINE. An ecological study of three-year-olds at home. Nashville, George Peabody College for Teachers, Nov. 7, 1969.

SHAW, JEAN W., & SCHOGGEN, MAXINE. Children learning: Samples of everyday life of children at home. The Demonstration and Research Center for Early Education, George Peabody College for Teachers, 1969.

SHEPARD, R. Recognition memory for words, sentences, and pictures. *Journal of Verbal Learning and Verbal Behavior*, 1967, *6*, 156–163.

SILBERMAN, C. *Crisis in the classroom.* New York: Random House, 1970.

SIMON, H. A. The architecture of complexity. *Proceedings of the American Philosophical Society*, 1962, *106*(6), 467–482.

SLOBIN, D. I. Questions of language development in cross-cultural perspective.

Paper prepared for symposium on "Language learning in cross-cultural perspective," Michigan State University, September 1968.

SMILANSKY, S. The effect of certain learning conditions on the progress of disadvantaged children of kindergarten age. *Journal of School Psychology,* Spring 1968, *4*(3).

SMITH, H. C. Age differences in color discrimination. *Journal of General Psychology,* 1943, *29,* 191–226.

SONTAG, L. W., BAKER, C. T., & NELSON, V. L. Mental growth and personality development: A longitudinal study. In Monographs of the Society for Research in Child Development, 1958, *23*(2).

STODOLSKY, S. S., & LESSER, G. S. Learning patterns in the disadvantaged. *Harvard Educational Review,* 1967, *37,* 546–593.

STRANDBERG, T. E., & GRIFFITH, J. A study of the effects of training in visual literacy on verbal language behavior. Eastern Illinois University, 1968.

STRODTBECK, F. L. Considerations of meta-method in cross-cultural studies. In A. K. Romney & R. G. D'Andrade (Eds.), Transcultural studies in cognition. *American Anthropologist,* Special Publication, 1964, *66,* 223–229.

STURTEVANT, W. C. Studies in ethnoscience. In A. K. Romney & R. G. D'Andrade (Eds.), Trans-cultural studies in cognition, *American Anthropologist,* Special Publication, 1964, *66,* 99–131.

SUGARMAN, J. M. *The future of early childhood programs: An American perspective.* Draft of book to be published, 1970.

TOLMAN, E. C. Cognitive maps in rats and men. *Psychological Review,* 1948, *55*(4), 189–204.

TOUGH, JOAN. An interim report of a longitudinal study. University of Leeds, Institute of Education, Language, and Environment, 1970.

TUCKER, A. W. Observations on the color vision of school children. *British Journal of Psychology,* 1911, *4,* 33–43.

TURNER, G. J., & PICKVANCE, R. E. Social class differences in the expression of uncertainty in five-year-old children. Sociological Research Unit, University of London, Institute of Education, 1970.

VAN DE GEER, J. P., & FRIJDA, N. H. Codability and recognition: An experiment with facial expressions. *Acta Psychologica,* Amsterdam, 1961, *18,* 360–367.

VYGOTSKY, L. *Thought and language.* (Ed. & trans. by Eugenia Hanfmann & Gertrude Vakar.) Cambridge, Mass.: MIT Press, and New York: Wiley, 1962.

WASHBURN, S. L. The analysis of primate evolution with particular reference to the origin of man. *Cold Spring Harbor Symposia on Quantitative Biology,* 1951, *XV,* 67–78.

WASHBURN, S. L. Behavior and the origin of man. *The Rockefeller University Review,* Jan.-Feb. 1968, 10–19.

WASHBURN, S. L., & HOWELL, F. C. Human evolution and culture. In S. Tax (Ed.), *Evolution of man.* Chicago: Univer. Chicago Press, 1960, 33–56.

WERNER, H. *Comparative psychology of mental development.* Chicago: Follet, 1948.

WHITE, R. W. Motivation reconsidered: The concept of competence. *Psychological Review,* 1959, *66,* 297–333.

WHITEHEAD, A. N. *The aims of education and other essays.* New York: Macmillan, 1929.

WHORF, B. L. *Language, thought, and reality.* J. B. Carroll (Ed.), Cambridge, Mass.: MIT Press, and New York: Wiley, 1956.

WINTRINGER, J. Considerations sur l'intelligence du Noir africain. *Revue de Psychologie des Peuples,* 1955, *10,* 37–55.

WITTGENSTEIN, L. *Philosophical investigations.* (Trans. G. E. M. Anscombe.) New York: Macmillan, 1959.

ZIGLER, E., & BUTTERFIELD, E. Motivational aspects of changes in IQ test performance of culturally deprived nursery school children. *Child Development,* 1968, *39*(1), 1–14.

A SELECTED BIBLIOGRAPHY OF WORKS
OF RELATED INTEREST BY THE AUTHOR

1939. McCulloch, T. L., and Bruner, J. S. The effect of electric shock upon subsequent learning in the rat. *Journal of Psychology* 7: 333–36.

1946. Bruner, J. S., and Brown, J. L. Contemporary France and educational reform. *Harvard Educational Review* 16: 10–20.

1947. Bruner, J. S., and Goodman, C. C. Value and need as organizing factors in perception. *Journal of Abnormal and Social Psychology* 42: 33–44.

1948. Bruner, J. S., and Postman, L. An approach to social perception. In *Current trends in social psychology,* ed. W. Dennis. Pittsburgh: U. of Pittsburgh Pr.

1948. Postman, L., Bruner, J. S., and McGinnies, E. Personal values as selective factors in perception. *Journal of Abnormal and Social Psychology* 43: 142–54.

1949. Postman, L., and Bruner, J. S. Multiplicity of set as a determinant of perceptual behavior. *Journal of Experimental Psychology* 39 (3): 369–77.

1949. Bruner, J. S., and Postman, L. On the perception of incongruity: a paradigm. *Journal of Personality,* 18 (2): 206–23.

1949. ———. Perception, cognition and behavior. *Ibid.* 18 (1): 14–31.

1951. Bruner, J. S. Personality dynamics and the process of perceiving. In *Perception—an approach to personality,* eds. R. R. Blake and G. Ramsey. New York: Ronald.

1951. Postman, L., Bruner, J. S., and Walk, R. D. The perception of error. *British Journal of Psychology* 42: 1–10.

1952. Postman, L., and Bruner, J. S. Hypothesis and the principle of closure: the effect of frequency and recency. *Journal of Psychology* 33: 113–25.

1954. Bruner, J. S., and Tagiuri, R. The perception of people. In *Handbook of social psychology,* ed. G. Lindzey. Reading, Mass.: Addison-Wesley.

1955. Bruner, J. S., Matter, J., and Papanek, M. L. Breadth of learning as a function of drive level and mechanization. *Psychological Review* 62 (1): 1–10.

1955. Bruner, J. S., Miller, G. A., and Zimmerman, C. Discriminative skill and discriminative matching in perceptual recognition. *Journal of Experimental Psychology* 49: 187–92.

1955. Bruner, J. S., and Minturn, A. L. Perceptual identification and perceptual organization. *Journal of General Psychology* 53: 21–28.

1956. Bruner, J. S. Freud and the image of man. *American Psychologist* 11 (9): 463–66.

1956. Bruner, J. S., Goodnow, J. J., and Austin, G. A. *A study in thinking.* New York: Wiley. (Paperback, New York: Wiley, 1962.)

1957. Bruner, J. S. Going beyond the information given. *Contemporary approaches to cognition,* eds. H. Gruber *et al.* Cambridge: Harvard U. Pr.

1957. ———. Mechanism riding high: Review of *Behavior theory and conditioning,* by K. W. Spence. *Contemporary Psychology* 2 (6): 155–57.

1957. ———. Neural mechanisms in perception. *Psychological Review* 64 (6): 340–58.

1957. ———. On perceptual readiness. *Ibid.* 64 (2): 123–52.

1957. ———. What social scientists say about having an idea. *Printers' Ink,* July 12, 260 (2): 48–52.

1958. Bruner, J. S., Mandler, J. M., O'Dowd, D., and Wallach, M. A. The role of overlearning and drive level in reversal learning. *Journal of Comparative and Physiological Psychology* 51 (5): 607–13.

1959. Bruner, J. S. The cognitive consequences of early sensory deprivation. *Psychosomatic Medicine* 21 (2): 89–95.

1959. ———. Learning and thinking. *Harvard Educational Review* 29 (3): 184–92.

1959. ———. A psychologist's viewpoint: Review of *The growth of logical thinking,* by B. Inhelder and J. Piaget. *British Journal of Psychology* 50: 363–70.

1959. Bruner, J. S., Galanter, E. H., and Wallach, M. A. The identification of recurrent regularity. *American Journal of Psychology* 72: 200–209.

1960. Bruner, J. S. The functions of teaching. *Rhode Island College Journal* 1: 2.

1960. ———. *The process of education.* Cambridge: Harvard U. Pr. (Paperback, New York: Vintage, 1963.)

1961. ———. The act of discovery. *Harvard Educational Review* 31: 21–32.

1961. ———. Affrontement et défense. *Journal de Psychologie Normale et Pathologique* (France) 1: 33–56.

1961. ———. After John Dewey, what? *Saturday Review* (Educational Supplement), June 17, 1961, p. 58.

1962. ———. Introduction: the new educational technology. *American Behavioral Scientist* 4 (3): 5.

1962. ———. *On knowing: essays for the left hand.* Cambridge: Harvard U. Pr. (Paperback. New York: Atheneum, 1965).

1963. Bruner, J. S. Looking at the curriculum. *The Educational Courier* (Toronto) 33 (3): 18–26.

1963. ———. Structures in learning. *NEA Journal* 52 (3): 26–27.

1964. Bruner, J. S. The course of cognitive growth. *American Psychologist* 19: 1–15.

1964. ———. Education as social invention. *Journal of Social Issues* 20 (3): 21–33.

1964. ———. Growing. In *Proceedings of the 1963 Invitational Conference on Testing Problems*, pp. 86–98. Princeton: Educational Testing Service.

1964. ———. Some theorems on instruction illustrated with reference to mathematics. In *Theories of learning and instruction*, eds. E. Hilgard & H. Richey. *Yearbook Nat. Soc. Stud. Educ.* 63: 305–35.

1965. ———. The growth of mind. *American Psychologist* 20: 1007–17.

1965. ———. Man: a course of study. *ESI Quarterly Report*, Spring–Summer, pp. 3–13.

1965. Bruner, J. S., and Kenney, H. J. Representation and mathematics learning. *Child Development Monograph*, Serial 99, 30 (1): 50–59.

1966. Bruner, J. S. *Toward a theory of instruction.* Cambridge: Harvard U. Pr. (Paperback, New York: Norton, 1968).

1966. ———. The will to learn. *Commentary* 41, no. 2; 41–46.

1966. Bruner, J. S., Ed. *Learning about learning: a conference report.* Washington, D.C.: U.S. Government Printing Office.

1966. Bruner, J. S., Olver, R. R., Greenfield, P. M., et al. *Studies in cognitive growth.* New York: Wiley.

1968. Bruner, J. S. Culture, politics, and pedagogy. *Saturday Review*, May 1968, p. 69.

1968. ———. *Processes of cognitive growth: infancy.* Heinz Werner Lecture Series, vol. 3. Worcester, Mass.: Clark U. Pr. with Barre.

1968. ———. Review of *Six psychological studies*, by Jean Piaget. *New York Times Book Review*, Feb. 11, 1968. Pp. 6 & 45.

1969. Bruner, J. S., and Bruner, B. M. On voluntary action and its hierarchical structure. In *Beyond reductionism*, eds. A. Koestler and J. S. Smythies. London: Hutchinson.

1969. Bruner, J. S. Processes of growth in infancy. In *Stimulation in early infancy*, ed. A. Ambrose. London: Academic Press.

1970. ———. *Poverty and childhood.* Detroit: Merrill-Palmer Institute.

1970. ———. Infant education as viewed by a psychologist. In *Education of the infant and young child*, ed. V. H. Denenberg. New York: Academic Press.

INDEX

Achievement motivation, 140–41
Action, *see* Learning
Agassis, Joseph, 116
Aims of Education, The, 15
Allport, Gordon W., 23, 55
Analysis, intuition and, 82, 83, 85–88
  see also Language
Anglin, J., 130
Animism, 26–27, 28
Art, 104–5, 107
Austin, G. A., 126, 146

Baker, C. T., 141
Baratz, S. S. and J. C., 152
Barker, Roger, 66
Bartlett, Sir Frederic, 37n, 55, 112
Bayley, Nancy, 141
Bee, Helen, 140, 142, 151
Bellugi, U., 151
Bernstein, Basil, 142, 148, 149
Bernstein, N., 127
Biesheuvel, S., 48, 51n
Bloom, B., 61, 133
Boas, F., 21
Bogoras, W. G., 23
Bohr, Niels, 17
Bonte, M., 23
Bouterline-Young, H., 141
Broder, L., 61
Brown, Roger, 36, 38, 41, 44, 146, 151, 152
Bruner, J. S., 22, 24, 25, 28, 37, 40, 41, 45, 48, 49, 124, 125, 126, 127, 133, 146, 147n, 153
Butler, R. A., 55

Cambridge Conference on School Mathematics (1963), 106
Carroll, J. B., 36
Casagrande, J. B., 36
Cazden, C. B., 146, 151
Césaire, Aimé, 34
Children, pre-school age,
  early education of, 134; achievement motivation and, 140–41
  formative years of, importance to intellectual achievement, 132–33
  infant learning, 129–31, 137–38
  maternal variables affecting intellectual achievement, 139–40, 142–43
  poverty and intellectual development of: cultural theories affecting, 153–54; curriculum reforms, 158–60; decentration and analytic capacity, 147; general discussion, 132, 133–35; goal seeking and problem solving, 135–43,

149; intervention, programs of, 156–58; language and, 134–35, 142–50; schooling and pre-schooling training, substandard quality of 154–55; sense of powerlessness, urbanization and, 141–42; social and educational inequities affecting, 133, 154–55; social reciprocity, and, 135, 150–53
Clark, W. E. L., 119, 121
Cognitive growth, *see* Culture
Cole, M., 33, 147n, 153
Coleman Report (1966), 153
Competence, *see* Learning
Concept(s),
  equivalence rule of, 25
  formation, 25, 26, 75
  formulation, 15
  as mental tools, 71–72
  see also Learning
Conservation, 25–26, 28–30, 31, 32, 33
Covington, M. V., 95, 127
Crutchfield, R. S., 95, 127
Cryns, A. G. J., 22, 48
Culture, 113
  amplification of skills and knowledge through, 52–53
  cognitive development and: approaches to study of, 20–24; biological factors affecting, 49–51; conservation experiments concerning, 25–26, 28–30, 31, 32, 33; equivalence experiments concerning, 25–26, 27, 42; heredity *v.* environment question, 20–21, 22, 50–51, 153–54; language factors involved, 21, 23, 34–48, 50; perceptual variations, 22–23; value orientation, 24–34
  comunal intellect, 7
  intellectual development theories, poverty and, 153–54
  and method of discovery in education, 68–69
  power and substance of, translation into instructional form, 105–7
  range of acceptable means within, 99
  reciprocal patterns of (Lévi-Strauss), 124–25
  "teaching the," 12
  see also Instruction; School/Schooling
Curriculum, *see* School/Schooling

Dart, R., 119
Darwin, Charles, 9
Davies, L. B., 95, 127

171